HEALTH INSURANCE SECTOR IN INDIA

HEALTH INSURANCE SECTOR IN INDIA

T. MAHENDRAN

ABHIJEET PUBLICATIONS

DELHI 110094

ABHIJEET PUBLICATIONS
2/46 Tukhmeerpur Extension
Delhi-110 094
Phone: 011-22960492, 65698474
E-mail: abhijeetpublication@gmail.com

HEALTH INSURANCE SECTOR IN INDIA

First Published 2008

ISBN 978-81-89886-87-5

PRINTED IN INDIA

Published by J.K. Singh for Abhijeet Publications, Delhi-110 094, Lasertypeset by Gaurav Graphics, New Delhi and Printed at Himanshu Printers, Delhi.

Dedicated

to

My Parents

C. THIAGARAJAN

& SUSHEELA

Preface

In the realm of globalization, many more multi-national corporations have entered into the field of insurance sector for the purpose of extending medical facilities and also enhancing better living conditions to the people. India has made considerable progress in improving the health status of her population. There is a considerate declining rate of crude death rate, due to better medical facilities. The World Health Organization has recommended a minimum of five percentage of GDP to health sector, but the real figure in India is very dismayed.

This book tries to bring out the developments in Health Insurance Sector in India in the post-liberaisation era.

To thank profusely scholars and authorities is a pleasure indeed.

I am greatly indebted to Dr. A. Arunachalam, M.A., M.Phil., M.L., Ph.D., M.B.A., Chairman and

Correspondent of Adaikalamatha College, Vallam, Thanjavur.

I owe my sincere thanks to respected Principal Dr. R. KATHIAN, M.Com., M.Phil., Ph.D., for his timely help.

I take this opportunity to express my heart felt thanks to my beloved Professors Dr. M. Perumal, Dr. V. Ethiraj (Retd.) Professor and Head of the Department of Ecionomics, AVVM Sri Pushpam College, Poondi, Prof. R. Rajendran, M.A., M.Phil., Ph.D., R.R. Palanivelu, Dept. of Economics, Pushpam College, Poondi, and other Department staffs.

I thank my wife without their constant pressure and co-operation.

I will failing in my duties, if I could express my profound thanks to my son for their. timely help in bringing his book in time.

I am thankful to Abhijeet Publications, Delhi for their Interest and co-operation in publishing this book.

I do not claim that could cover all the aspects of the Perspective Health Insurance within the limited space, but I firmly believe that this book will be very useful to all concerned.

T.MAHENDRAN

Thanjavur,

June 2008

Contents

1

Health Insurance and Third Party Administrators: Issues and Challenges

Introduction

Efficient and effective healthcare is determined by the way the financing of healthcare systems is structured and organized. The health financing system in India is dependent on government budgetary allocations and private financing. The role of the latter has increased significantly in recent years. Most of it is 'out-of-pocket' private expenditure, which has grown at the rate of 12.5 per cent, and for each 1 per cent increase in per capita income it has increased by about 1.44 per cent [Bhat 1999]. In the absence of effective regulation of private health services, healthcare costs are inevitably high, and it is people belonging to the lower income classes who suffer the most. In recent times, healthcare has become almost unaffordable and has given rise to serious equity issues. Hence it is imperative that we find alternative health financing mechanisms. Health insurance is one such alternative.

Health insurance protects people against catastrophic financial burden resulting from unexpected illness or injury. An efficient system ensures the pooling of resources to cover risks. Health insurance in India is at a nascent stage and contributes to a small proportion of the health expenditure. The government, through its state-run schemes such as the Employee State Insurance Scheme (ESIS), Central Government Health Scheme (CGHS), and the Mediclaim scheme offered by government-run insurance companies, has played a significant role. NGOs and community-based Organizations such as SEWA too offer a number of schemes for the poor and vulnerable groups to meet the high cost of healthcare. Recently, the government allowed private insurance companies to offer health insurance products.

Under the existing private medical insurance scheme, which is indemnity based, policy-holders, at the time of needing healthcare services, first pay for the expenses and are only later reimbursed, depending on the sum insured and the coverage. Besides having cost escalating characteristics, these schemes are inefficient and have a number of limitations. Insurance companies have to deal with unregulated healthcare providers who work in an environment where there are no standards, quality benchmarks and treatment protocols, and where highly variable billing systems and significant price variations across providers exist (reflected by the adverse claim ratios). It has also been observed that hospitals tend to overcharge the patients covered by insurance, but in the absence of monitoring and control mechanisms, it is difficult to handle fraudulent claims. It is to address such issues that insurance intermediaries such as third party administrators (TPAs) become important and they are bound to play a key role in the growth and development of a managed healthcare system. TPAs are separate entities who coordinate between insurance companies, customers and healthcare providers; they arrange for cashless hospitalisation and closely monitor the use of resources and services. Health insurance companies generally tie up with TPAs for the back-office function of managing claims and reimbursements. IRDA has also come up with regulatory guidelines for TPAs, which have to fulfil certain requirements and observe a code of conduct.

The objective of this paper is to discuss the role and importance of TPAs in the emerging health insurance market in India. The paper specifically aims to:

- understand the functioning of TPAs in health insurance
- analyse the existing TPA system
- examine issues and challenges TPAs face in an unregulated health sector
- analyse IRDA regulations on TPA and their implications.

The paper is divided into six sections. Section II gives the salient features of the healthcare system and health financing in India. Section III explains the health insurance system and the current scenario in health insurance. Section IV discusses the concept of managed care. Section V describes TPA and its functioning. Section

VI discusses IRDA regulations and their impact, regulatory issues, and the prospect of intermediaries in the Indian insurance sector.

Indian Healthcare System

India has made considerable progress in improving the health status of its population. Crude death rate has fallen from about 40 per 1,000 at the time of independence to 9 per 1,000 in 1998, which can be attributed to the mortality reduction of the under five age group from around 161 per 1,000 live births to 71 over the same period. Consequently, life expectancy has increased from about 31 years to 63 years. Yet challenges remain: life expectancy is still four years below the world average and under-five mortality (12 per 1,000 per year) is higher than the world average.

India is one of the major countries where communicable diseases are still not under control: polio has not yet been eradicated, HIV incidence is on the increase and tuberculosis and malaria still take a high toll. Chronic non-communicable diseases such as heart disease, diabetes, and cancer are also on the rise. The health sector, therefore, faces dual challenges: while the control of communicable diseases is of paramount importance, non-communicable diseases should be addressed as well (for instance, the incidence of diabetes and heart disease in India is double that of China). The primary healthcare system is not yet geared to diagnose and treat chronic degenerative diseases. India, therefore, faces the daunting challenge of meeting healthcare needs of its population and ensuring accessibility, efficiency, equity, and quality of healthcare.

Through its budgetary allocations the government

has set up remarkably impressive health infrastructure. The system envisages availability and accessibility of publicly funded healthcare to all, regardless of their ability to pay. However, it faces serious challenges in meeting its objectives.

The present healthcare system is characterised by mixed ownership patterns and different types of providers who practice different systems of medicine. Both public and private facilities provide health services, but the bulk of the curative services is skewed towards the urban areas and dominated by the private sector.

Public Health Sector: The Bhore Ccommittee, set up in 1946, set the foundation for the current public healthcare system. The Committee recommended free healthcare funded by the state, with general and local taxation generating funds to provide for it. The government provides medical care through government-run hospitals, dispensaries, primary health centres, sub-centres, and other health facilities. Primary care consists of health centres and dispensaries where basic medical treatment for common ailments is provided, as also immunisation and health promotional activities. Secondary medical care is provided by specialists at the district, sub-divisional, and community health centre level. Tertiary medical care is provided by super specialists at multi-specialty, and super-specialty hospitals and medical colleges. Research, training, and education are also carried out at tertiary levels. State governments own the bulk of the health delivery system and have to bear the costs of operation. Government hospitals account for 30 per cent of hospitals and 60 per cent of beds, whereas local bodies own 2 per cent of hospitals and 3 per cent of beds. State-owned enterprises like Coal India, railways and the police have developed their own healthcare facilities.

Private Health Sector: The private sector plays an important role in India's health delivery system and has a wide network of facilities that cater to the requirements of both urban and rural populations. The presence of the private sector has profound implications for the existing character of the Indian healthcare system, since it affects both cost and quality of services available [Bhat 1996]. The private sector consists of organized private and voluntary institutions, accounting for 68 per cent of the hospitals and 37 per cent of hospital beds. Variations in hospitals and beds are quite significant across states. The organized private sector is primarily profit-oriented and includes all levels of private hospitals, dispensaries, nursing homes, general practitioners and pharmacies. The voluntary, not-profit institutions are run by charitable trusts. About 10 per cent of hospitals and 13 per cent of hospital beds are in the voluntary sector. The informal private sector consists of practitioners with no formal qualifications and various types of less-qualified providers. Surveys show that a majority of people seek care from private providers. Concern about quality of public services is the main reason for this.

Healthcare Financing

Current health expenditure in India is estimated to be around Rs. 1,030 billion. India spends 6 per cent of its GDP on health. The share of government is less than 2 per cent [Tulasidhar 1992]. The World Health Organization has recommended that governments must spend at least 5 per cent of GDP on the health sector.

The bulk of healthcare spending is direct out-of-pocket household expenditure (Table 1).

Though the demand for healthcare is increasing owing to population pressure, the government is finding it very difficult to maintain its health facilities. Government allocations have also been declining over the years (Table 2).

Government allocations in the health sector have declined from 1.3 per cent of GDP in 1990 to 0.9 per cent in 1999 (National Health Policy, 2001). The central government plays an important role in supporting national health programmes such as malaria, TB and HIV/AIDS. Funds for these programmes are channel through the state governments. These schemes give priority to primary healthcare. Where as state governments bear the major responsibility of recurrent costs, especially the cost of running the hospitals. The significance of alternative sources of financing has increased. There are four major alternatives for mobilising resources other than government funds.

Table 1: National Health Spending- Sources & Uses

(Per cent)

	Central Govt.	*State Govt.*	*Corporate 3rd Party*	*Households Out-of-Pocket*	*Total*
Primary care	4.3	5.6	0.8	48	58.7
Secondary & tertiary	0.9	8.4	2.5	27	38.8
Inpatient care					
Non-service Provision	0.9	1.6	na	na	2.5
Total	6.1	15.6	3.3	75	100

Table 2: Health Expenditure as Percentage of GSDP of the States

States	*1990-91*	*1991-92*	*1992-93*	*1993-94*	*1994-95*	*1995-96*	*1996-97*	*Avg*	*(7)-(1)*
Andhra Pradesh	0.94	0.90	0.95	0.96	0.90	0.84	0.95	0.92	0.01
Assam	1.04	1.20	1.05	1.17	1.16	1.23	1.20	1.15	0.16
Biha	1.03	0.99	1.12	0.99	1.00	1.21	1.04	1.05	0.01
Gujarat	0.90	0.93	0.78	0.80	0.71	0.77	0.72	0.80	-0.18
Haryana	0.60	0.58	0.62	0.60	0.58	0.58	0.55	0.59	-0.05
Karnataka	1.04	0.98	1.09	1.03	1.03	0.98	0.93	1.01	-0.12
Kerala	1.51	1.27	1.15	1.26	1.27	1.32	1.30	1.30	-0.21
Madhya Pradesh	0.90	0.94	0.92	0.91	0.91	0.84	0.87	0.90	-0.04
Maharashtra	0.74	0.72	0.68	0.65	0.61	0.60	0.59	0.66	-0.15
Orissa	1.24	1.12	1.13	1.08	1.06	1.06	1.07	1.11	-0.17
Punjab	0.88	0.79	0.75	0.72	0.64	0.64	0 68	0.73	-0.20
Rajasthan	1.21	1.21	1.23	1.35	1.32	1.33	1.24	1.27	-0.03
Tamil Nadu	1.21	1.15	1.14	1.06	1.00	1.03	0.99	1.08	-0.22
Uttar Pradesh	1.12	0.97	1.04	1.16	1.00	1.00	0.99	1.04	-0.13
West Bengal	1.24	0.96	0.99	1.02	0.88	0.90	0.90	0.98	-0.34

Community Financing: Individuals, families or community groups make voluntary contributions towards meeting healthcare costs. The cost is shared among members regardless of individual use. This works out well for small groups.

User Fee: This is fee paid for services or out-of-pocket expenses from users. This helps in improving revenue and rationalises utilization in government systems. However, fee-for service in the unregulated health sector has many perverse incentives. Employer-based: The corporate sector or employers provide healthcare facilities to employees or reimburse healthcare expenses.

Health Insurance: Health insurance is a mechanism of pooling resources and sharing risks or uncertainties among many people. It ensures some form of equity. The focus is on contributory arrangements.

The private out-of-pocket expenses borne by households make up most of the health expenditure, accounting for more than 75 per cent of the total. Only 3 to 4 per cent of healthcare provision is funded through prepayment schemes and third parties such as corporations.

Most of the budgetary allocation by the government is for preventive, promotive and primary care and curative services, whereas private expenditure is largely on curative services. Private healthcare expenditure has grown at a rate of 12.84 per cent annually and for each 1 per cent increase in per capita income private healthcare expenditure has increased by 1.47 per cent [Bhat 1996].

Health Insurance

Insurance provides protection against risks or uncertain events and is based on the principle that what is highly unpredictable to an individual is predictable to a group of individuals. Health insurance protects against the cost of illness, mobilises funds for health services, increases the efficiency of mobilisation of funds and provision of health services, and achieves certain equity objectives [Mills 2000]. Various forms of health insurance can be broadly categorised (based on ownership of scheme) as follows: state-based systems, market-based systems, member Organization (NGO or cooperative)-based systems, and private household-based systems [Jutting 1999].

Social health insurance: Organized by the state or a public body, funding comes from payroll taxes levied on workers and employers, and often supplemented by user fees and government contributions from tax revenues. A wide range of benefits is offered but access is based on healthcare need. Social insurance schemes are managed by autonomous bodies under government regulations and the providers of care have to meet certain standards in terms of capacity, staff, equipment, and other parameters.

Private insurance: Both individuals and groups can avail of this voluntary coverage, which could be profit or non-profit oriented. Contributions are based on risk and coverage; benefits are specifically defined in this type of insurance.

Community-Based Insurance: Expenditure is shared among the community and generally community Organizations or NGO handle the business. Contributions can be mandatory or voluntary, usually a flat rate per individual or household. Health insurance is complex and there are serious market failure problems. In any market-driven system, what should be produced, how should it be produced and for whom it should be produced are determined by market forces. Competitive environments take care that resources are used efficiently (a lowest cost) and effectively (with optimum outcomes). However because of various demand and supply-side imperfections, there are inherent problems in health insurance markets. Important constraints on insurance contracts are [Burgess and Stern 1991]

- moral hazard;
- adverse selection;
- covariate risks; and
- information problems.

Moral Hazard: A serious problem, it arises because policy holder would like to take decisions and actions which maximise their benefit and do not want to bear the full cost. The seminal works of Arrow (1963) and Pauly (1968, 1974), who proposed the moral hazard problem in medical care suggest that the policyholder does not consider the insurer's costs. Unregulated healthcare market and private insurance encourage this behaviour since insurance lowers or avoids the cost of treatment at the point of treatment consumers tend to demand more (consumer moral hazard) Providers have an incentive to render more or unnecessary cart than might be medically appropriate (provider induced moral hazard). To combat this problem, most insurance companies use mechanisms and conditionalities which in the end only burden policyholders with part of cost [Sonderstrom 1997]. Some of the mechanisms insurance companies have adopted are co-payment, or co-insurance, deductibles, or a reduced premium bonus for the future. Another possibility of coping with moral hazard is to arrange special contracts [Jutting 1999].

Adverse Selection: The works of Akerlof (1970), Spence (1973), Stiglitz (1975), and Rothschild and Stiglitz (1976) have pioneered the concept of the adverse selection problem. Adverse selection arises when persons belonging to high-risk, groups seek coverage and the insurer cannot identify the risk. All policy holders are required to pay the same premium, whereas those belonging to higher-risk groups are likely to consume higher than the average quantity of services; they will also find the insurance policy more attractive, while those with good health will find insurance premium too high. Fewer and fewer, good cases will enroll in the insurance scheme and, as a result, the insurer fined having a pool of more risk cases. As Newberry and Stiglitz (1981) and Newberry (1989) have shown, insurance pools work best with easily identifiable risks.

Covariate Risks: The basic objective of any insurance mechanism is to protect individuals from risk. In most situations, the insured helps in protecting policyholders from unique health risks, and it is expected that these risks are not related to others in the insurance pool. However, if covariate or collective risks—possible risks that would cause damage to many or even all members on the pool at the same time [Jutting 1999] — occur, there is nothing to be gained by cooperation [Sonderstrom 1997]. The stronger the degree of positive covariance, the higher will be the cost whereas negatively correlated risks will have the effect of reducing the total cost of risk-bearing [Platteau 1991]. High incidence and prevalence of communicable diseases in a community can give rise to high covariate risks. In a study of claims and reimbursements, about 22 per cent of the cases arose from communicable diseases [Bhat and Reuben 2002]. In India, 50 per cent of deaths take place because of communicable diseases. If all policyholders face similar risks, the risk cannot DC reduced much through having insurance [Jutting 1999].

Information Problem: Availability of information would have a significant bearing on the development of insurance contracts. The severity of a moral hazard problem and adverse selection problems will depend on differences in the availability of-information between insurer and policyholders. In order to address this problem, insurance companies need significant investments in infrastructure and development of systems.

How, do these different forms of insurance address the risks? Each insurance setting has its strengths and weaknesses [Jutting 1999] as summarised in Table 3.

Features of Health Insurance and Indian Scenario

Reimbursement System: This system refers to the manner in which providers are paid. The characteristics of health insurance programme can be described as follows [Kutzin and Barnum 1992]:

In the traditional indemnity system, customers first incur Expenditure on services and later submit claim to insurance company for reimbursement (such as, Mediclaim insurance scheme).

- Managed indemnity in which a third party administrator (TPA) takes care of the claim settlement of enrolees and directly reimburses service provider.

- Insurer pays service provider a fixed amount, out of which provider will serve health needs of enrolees for a specific period.
- Reimbursement can be fee-for-service, which would involve charging for each individual service, such as inpatient bed-days, drugs, investigations.
- Case-specific reimbursement based on category of patient admitted. Under this system admissions are grouped into categories called diagnostic-related groups (DRGs), based on their clinical characteristics.

Services covered by insurance: Coverage of services varies with each insurance programme. Some cover only curative services whereas others cover primary OPD care too. Coverage varies according to the extent of hospitalisation also.

Role of the insurer: The insuring institution can play either an inactive or a passive role. If it is a mere funding entity and is not directly involved in the provision of healthcare services, controlling of costs becomes difficult. It develops mechanisms of cost sharing to mitigate the negative impacts, and beneficiaries are asked to pay an amount each time they use the services as deductibles (the insured pays a specific amount before receiving insurance benefits) or co-payment (a fixed percentage of cost; of service is paid by the beneficiary to the insurance company). On the other hand, if the insurance company is a managed care Organization (directly involved in organising and providing healthcare services), it can enforce cost discipline more rigorously.

The promulgation of the Employee State Insurance (ESI) Act in 1948 ushered in health insurance in India.

The legislation introduced a mandatory social insurance scheme with managed care concepts for employees in the formal sector. The Employee State Insurance Scheme (ESIS), introduced in 1952, is managed by the Employees State Insurance Corporation (ESIC), a wholly government owned enterprise. It provides cash benefits, medical benefits, preventive and promotive care, and health education. It is a compulsory social security benefit for workers having an income less than Rs 6.500 a month in the formal sector, covers employees and their dependants and is mainly financed by contributions from employers, employees and the government. Employers and employees contribute 4.75 per cent and 1.75 per cent of their wages respectively. The state government's share is 12.5 per cent of the total expenditure. In 2000, about 33.4 million beneficiaries were covered by the scheme. ESIC has set up 136 hospitals with 43 annexes having 23,720 beds. There are 1,443 ESI dispensaries, 6,542 medical officers, and 2.988 medical practitioners.

The second initiative was the Central Government Health Scheme (CGHS) in 1954 for employees of the central government, members of parliament, judges, freedom fighters, and their families. Mainly financed by the central government, this contributory health scheme—contribution varies from Rs. 15 to Rs. 150 per person based on the salary of the employee—provides comprehensive medical care to about 4.4 million beneficiaries (1996 figure). Separate dispensaries are maintained and inpatient facilities are available in government hospitals and approved private hospitals on referral.

For persons not covered by these schemes, government-run insurance companies have introduced market-based schemes, such as the Mediclaim scheme of General Insurance Corporation, introduced in 1986. An indemnity-based health system, covering only inpatient treatment, the premium is based on age and sum insured. Clients can avail of medical services from any public or registered private hospital. In 1991, however, the internal limits for doctor's fee, medicines, diagnostics, and room charges were removed, making it a single benefit policy.

There are health benefit packages that are directly managed by employers in both the public and private sector: either special healthcare facilities are set up or reimbursement of medical expenses and Medical claim insurance premium amounts (often a group Medical claim scheme) can be claimed.

Many charitable and Voluntary Organizations have also designed social security schemes for specific groups of the population, and NGOs often provide some kind of social security to the poor and those working in the un organized sector, especially in rural areas. The Self Employed Women's Association (SEWA) has been in the forefront and other important Organizations such as Child in Need Institute, Streehitkarini, Tribhuvandas Foundation, and Accord have also taken the initiative.

Table 3: Strengths and Weakness

Risks & Concerns	*Insurance Settings Government*	*Market*	*Member*
Moral hazard	--	+	++
Adverse selection	+++	--	-
Covariate risks	+++	++	+/-
Cost efficiency	--	++	+/-
Quality	-	+++	+/-
Equity of access	++	---	++

Notes : + strong comparative advantage/strong disadvantage

Govt. : universal insurance run by government;

Market : private voluntary insurance;

Member : insurance systems run by member-based Organizations.

Source : Jutting (1999).

The government has now allowed private companies to enter into health insurance and has established the Insurance Regulatory and Development Authority (IRDA) to regulate this sector. It is estimated that the present health insurance market is Rs 2.5 bn-3bn and it has a potential to grow to Rs 50 billion in the next five to seven years. The potential insurable lives in the country are estimated to be around 300 million and only 10 per cent of the health insurance market has been tapped so far.

Managed Care

During the 1960s and 1970s, researchers in the US pointed out that: *(a)* health insurance motivates people to seek unnecessary health benefits (customer moral hazard), and *(b)* providers have a financial incentive to recommend the costliest of treatments (provider induced moral hazard or demand inducement), that have little or no impact on health outcomes [Dranove 2000]. These behaviours ultimately drive up costs without commensurate increase in the quality of care. Managed care Organizations came into existence in the US to contain the cost of healthcare under the insurance system and address the issue of dysfunctional fragmented services [Fairfield et al 1997].

Under managed care, health insurance companies establish linkages with healthcare providers and they in turn assume responsibility and accountability for the resources they use in providing healthcare services. Mechanisms which ensure that service providers share part of the financial risk inherent in assuming the responsibility have been developed and the goal is to provide quality care to policyholders. Special emphasis is placed on coordinated and comprehensive services, appropriate use of both ambulatory and inpatient settings, evidence-based decision-making, cost-effective diagnosis and treatment, population-based planning, and health promotion and disease prevention. Utilization review, case management, coordinated care, home healthcare, pharmacy benefit management, information technology systems, physician contracting, and network development are some of the features of managed care [ibid].

Cost control is achieved by fixing fees for services, monitoring the need for procedures such as tests and operations, and stressing on preventive care. The three dimensions of managed care are rules and policies, systems management including how policies and rules are administered, and disease management focusing on how diseases presenting to the system are dealt with.

Though the managed care concept was initiated in the US in the early part of the 20th century, it was the launch of the Kaiser Health Plan during second world war that resulted in the first clinic-based system of managed care. American employers offered workers 100 per cent coverage of healthcare costs with a variety benefits. During the 1960s, healthcare became more technology-intensive and highly specialised and with the introduction Medicare and Medicaid in the US, costs of medical services skyrocketed. The Health Maintenance Organization (HMO) Act of 1973 paved the way for managed care Organizations to become publicly funded companies, providing capital and accelerating their growth. The decade from 1985 to 1995 saw the proliferation of these Managed Care Organizations (MCOs) in an effort to contain escalating costs. Today, more than 90 per cent of the healthcare industry and three out of four US workers go through managed care Organizations.

Managed Care Organizations use utilization management strategies to control the use of services. The basic idea is to review and supervise expensive decisions, ensuring that they are in accord with the prescribed guidelines and treatment protocols utilization management is done through ensuring pre-certification of inpatient admissions for use of expensive technologies concurrent review of length of inpatient stay or other expensive courses of treatment, management of high-cost cases, and having a system of second opinion. Before admitting non-emergency patients to the hospital or undertaking other specified expensive treatments, doctors in managed care Organizations are required call the insurer's utilization Management Company and have the decision approved. After admission, utilization manager monitor the inpatient stay to ensure the earliest possible discharge. In complex or difficult cases, a case manager may work with the doctor to develop a treatment plan that substitutes less expensive care wherever possible. Utilization management seek to reduce healthcare costs by avoiding unnecessary hospital admissions and reducing the length of stay.

Managed care companies are able to reduce costs by negotiating aggressively with hospitals and provider groups on rates and, us of inexpensive resources in inpatient care.

Forms of Managed Care

Most managed care is carried out in one of two basic type of Organizational settings: health maintenance Organization (HMC) or preferred provider Organization (PPO).

Health Maintenance Organization: Considered the cheapest option HMOs insure and provide comprehensive medical services to voluntarily enrolled members on a prepaid basis. They own health facilities and employ health professionals to run them. Member are required to choose a primary care physician (PCP) whole they must consult for all their healthcare needs. The PCP typically authorises most referrals to specialists and other services. Customers pay a fixed fee for services —usually a monthly fee which remains the same regardless of services availed—instead of separate charges for visits or services.

HMOs can be grouped under four categories based on how the physicians are organized: staff model, group model, Independent practice association (IPA), and net work model. State model HMOs employ their own physicians, group model HMC are insurance companies that have contracts with large physicians groups to organize services. Physicians in staff and growth models often work exclusively for an HMO. IPAs and network model HMOs develop linkages with existing providers and agree to use their infrastructure. There are models that combine the features of IPAs and networks.

Preferred Provider Organization: Under PPO, health insurance companies contract with independent service providers, hospitals, and other healthcare professionals, who become the preferred or participating providers. Providers typically acce reduced, discounted fee-for-service rates of reimbursement from the health plan in exchange for access to the PPO's enrolee. The PPOs have fewer restrictions than HMOs. For example patients are not required to select a primary care physician seek prior authorisation for services, and may choose to receive care from other providers (who do not participate in the PPO with higher co-payments and deductibles attached to service provided by non-participating providers.

There are various variations of these arrangements. For example, point-of-service health plan (POS) combines the feature of an HMO with indemnity insurance option. Members use the plan like an HMO and receive HMO coverage, but may exercise freedom of choice and seek care outside the HMO system with additional charges (higher co-payments and deductibles, and submission of claims forms). They also choose how and from whom to receive services at the time they need them. Another variation is independent practice association (IPA), in which health care professionals maintain their own separate practices, while forming an MCO to contract with purchasers to provide are eat established rates. A third is physician hospital organization, (PHO), which is a legal entity formed and owned by one or more hospitals and physician groups in order to obtain payer contracts and to further mutual interests.

Managed care had its origin in the US, where a majority of the people are enrolled in some kind of managed care plan. Managed care Organizations such as HMOs and PPOs constitute 7 per cent of the American health insurance sector. It is estimated that managed care saves for patients over $300 billion annually and the quality is comparable to traditional indemnity insurance. More than 70 per cent of physicians in US work for MCOs. Clinicians are subject to prospective utilization reviews and pre-authorization requirements, concurrent reviews along with the treatment, retrospective reviews once treatment has been completed, and sometimes even mandatory second opinions. They have to follow clinical guidelines and their performance is continuously monitored and compared with that of their peers. Patients, however, do not trust managed care because they think that aggressive intervention by MCOs might limit the ability of their doctors to control and coordinate the resources necessary deliver quality care. Healthcare professionals also hold negative views towards managed care as physicians feel that it restricts their freedom of patient management [Simon 2001].

Figure 1: TPAS in Health Insurance

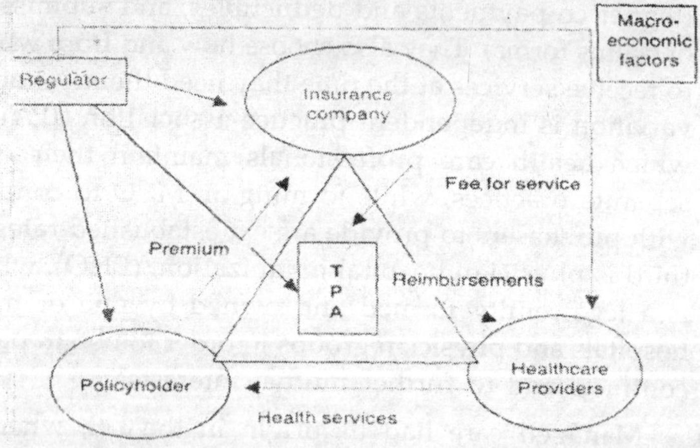

Managed care is new in Europe. European Organizations prefer integrated care or coordinated care instead of managed care because of its negative connotations in the US. However, they managed care as an absolute necessity for delivering quality.

Britain's largest private health insurer, BUPA, is adopting principles of US-style managed care, but this has brought widespread resistance from physicians, who fear that managed care will limit their freedom. In France, the first PPO was formed in 1995; in Holland, the first managed-care Organization was launched in 1997; and in Germany, health reforms in 1997 permitted pilot projects to use some aspects of managed care such as physician contracting. Germany provides healthcare through statutory medical insurance to 90 per cent of the population, but since costs are rising it has called for new alternative forms of controlled and organized healthcare based on the philosophy of managed care. Switzerland was the first European country to adopt managed care on a broad scale and has achieved considerable cost advantages from reduction in hospital stay.

While in the US, consumers argue that managed care limit's choice, in Europe the consumer experience is that private insurance increases their choices and decreases the waiting time typical of government-sponsored care. Providers in managed-care projects coordinate it so patients can obtain care at any hour of the day from a network physician [Katzman 1998].

In Asia, China opened up its insurance sector to foreign players in 1992. It concentrates on home care—quite different from managed care—which will curtail the rising cost of hospital care. Thailand introduced the concept of managed care in 1996. The Philippines allowed entry of foreign insurance companies in 1991 and the HMO concept seems to be well accepted. The concept of managed care is picking up in Singapore, Indonesia and Malaysia too. It is too early to assess the impact of managed care in these countries.

The Role of TPAs

Third Party Administrators (TPAs) are not technically Managed Care Organizations but play an important role in health insurance markets. Neither insurance companies nor care providers, they are intermediaries who bring together all components of healthcare, such as physicians, hospitals, clinics, long-term facilities, and pharmacies.

Their services include cashless service at hospitals, call centre support to policyholders, medical cost management, and management of claims and reimbursements. They also provide services to the corporate sector in designing and managing health benefit packages for their employees. Given the demand and supply-side complexities in health insurance and healthcare markets, TPAs provide an important link between insurance companies, healthcare providers and policyholders (Figure 1).

Intermediation by TPAs ensures that policyholders get hassle-free services; insurance companies pay for efficient and cost-effective services, and healthcare providers/policyholders get their reimbursements on time.

The core product or service of a TPA is ensuring cashless hospitalisation to policyholders. TPAs require skills to develop networks, manage finance, and delivery of appropriate healthcare services to its clients.

TPAs organise healthcare providers by establishing networks with hospitals, general practitioners, diagnostic centres, pharmacies, dental clinics, and physiotherapy clinics. They sign a memorandum of understanding with insurance companies according to which they inform policyholders about the network of healthcare delivery facilities and various systems and processes for settling claims. Policyholders are enrolled and registered with TPAs to avail of these services. In the event of hospitalisation, health facilities are expected to inform the TPAs. The medical referee of the TPA examines the admissibility of the case and accordingly informs the healthcare facility to proceed with the treatment.

The agreement between TPAs and healthcare facilities provides for monitoring and collection of documents and bills pertaining to the treatment. Documents are audited and after processing sent to the insurance company for reimbursement. TPAs have the responsibility of managing claims, getting reimbursements from the insurance company and paying the healthcare provider. Sometimes they pay the healthcare provider from the corpus amount without getting reimbursement from the insurance company.

With the routing of reimbursements through TPAs, the system has undergone a change. Earlier, clients were handling everything themselves and there were risks of delay in reimbursements and non-payments of some expenses incurred. But it is providers who now face the risk of not getting reimbursements from TPAs. Besides, once patients are admitted and if treatment costs exceed the sum insured, providers may not get the difference between the treatment cost and the sum-insured.

Range of Services Offered by Managed Care Organizations

As part of the agreement between healthcare providers and TPAs, some providers insist on getting a part of the expected costs as advance.

TPAs generally have in-house expertise of medical doctors, hospital managers, insurance consultants, legal experts, information technology professionals, and management consultants. The backbone of TPAs is information management system. Analysis of data regarding hospital admissions across the network (this also helps in identifying health needs and effective treatment protocols), analysis of treatment, tracking documents pertaining to each case, and tracking shortfalls in claims are essentials of claim management. Various functions of TPAs are summarised in Figure 2.

The client groups of TPAs can be divided into two broad categories: corporates and individuals/Often, the entire administration of medical facility and benefits for employees are handled and managed by TPAs who design and customise a policy according to the nature of health risks the employees face. Most TPAs operating in India focus on corporates.

Revenue Generation

The major source of revenue for TPAs is the fees charged for providing various services. Insurance companies pay the fee according to the volume and scope of services provided by them and it usually a fixed percentage of the premium collected from the enrolees. However, TPAs may provide many other services to Organizations for which the fee is paid by the Organization directly. These services include:

- *Benefit management:* TPAs help in designing appropriate health plans for the corporate sector and insurance companies.
- *Medical management:* This is basically disease management and involves medical follow-up of

the case. TPAs track the line of treatment and ensure genuine treatment.

- *Provider network management:* This is the key task. TPAs need to negotiate with service providers regarding quality of care, credit facility, discounts, package pricing, priority appointments and admissions. Periodic review and evaluation of the performance of service providers is also vital.
- *Claims administration:* This involves the claim adjudication process. The tasks include documentation, checking eligibility and coverage, claim submission and arranging payment for the service provider.
- *Information and data management:* TPAs can generate a lot of reports and database. These can be used as management tools for analysis and controlling cost and besides helping design new products.

Health insurance markets suffer from several shortcomings. The justification for introducing the TPA services is that they help minimize moral hazard. For this purpose, TPAs follow each case in an individualised way. TPAs do comprehensive review of records and maintain constant communication with healthcare providers and families. They also evaluate the outcome of treatment and have adequate data to compare it across different service providers. This knowledge base helps them to be more effective in handling future cases.

Value added services provided by TPAs may include arrangement of ambulance services, mediciftes and supplies, guide members for specialised consultation, provide information about health facilities, hospitals, bed availability, Organization of lifestyle management and well-being programmes, and 24 hour helplines.

TPAs are at a nascent stage in India. Managed care assumes critical significance in India as private practice and hospitals are not regulated and face a number of challenges. Considering current, trends most government-owned insurance companies offering Mediclaim insurance have started hiring TPAs. New entrants in health insurance will also find the services of TPAs important.

IRDA has made it mandatory for TPAs to acquire licence to operate in India. So far, IRDA has granted licence to 23 TPAs. TPAs have formed an association called the Indian Association of TPAs to organise themselves and protect their interests.

Regulatory Issues and Challenges

The effectiveness of TPAs in managing claims and reimbursements depends on their bargaining power vis-a-vis healthcare service providers. It is envisaged that TPAs can get better negotiated agreements with hospitals and medical practitioners and will introduce better monitoring system leading to lower claim ratios. However, in practice, there are many challenges which TPAs face in achieving these goals. The management of claims and reimbursements in highly fragmented, unregulated markets and dealing with a large number of small-sized service providers is bound to affect the revenue generation of TPAs. TPAs will be required to employ medical management experts and managers who can negotiate deals with a large number of service providers. Given that healthcare providers are not regulated and there is no information on various operational aspects of healthcare facilities such as occupancy rates, and length of stay, negotiating rates and levels of quality of care will be a tough task. The role of TPAs will still be in managing indemnity. Many concepts and mechanisms of managed care which help to contain costs are difficult to implement in current circumstances. For example, there is no system of capitation payment and therefore there is less scope to negotiate deals and get discounts in hospital charges.

The IRDA has approved services of TPAs as insurance intermediaries and would be regulating their practices, IRDA defines TPA as "an insurance intermediary licensed by the Authority who, either directly or indirectly, solicits or effects coverage of, underwrite, collect, charge premium from an insured, or adjust or settle claims in connection with health insurance, except as an agent or broker or an insurer." The final draft of these regulations has strictly barred TPAs from marketing health insurance products and charging the insured.

IRDA in consultation with the Insurance Advisory Committee has formulated the Insurance Regulatory and Development Authority (Third Party Administrators- Health Services) Regulations, 2001 to regulate TPA services. The salient features are as follows:

- Only an Organization registered under the Companies Act 1956 with a share capital of at least Rs 10 million in equity shares can set up a TPA in health services.
- TPA will be required to start with a minimum working capital of Rs 10 million at any point of functioning.
- The primary object of the company should be

to carry on business in India as a TPA in health services. It should not engage itself in any other business.

- At least one of the directors shall be a qualified medical doctor registered with the Medical Council of India. The CEO or CAO of the TPA should have successfully undergone a course in hospital management from an institution recognised by IRDA and have passed the licentiate examination conducted by the Insurance Institute of India, Mumbai. Apart from this, he should have undergone practical training of at least three months in the field of health management. TPAs should have access to competent medical professionals to advise insurance companies and clients on various matters.
- Foreign equity in TPAs is limited to 26 per cent. In case of any share transfer exceeding 5 per cent of paid-up capital, IRDA has to be informed within 15 days of such transfer.
- TPAs should obtain licence from IRDA to function. The application fee is Rs 20,000 and once the application is approved, another Rs 30,000 has to be paid as licensing fee. The licence will be renewed every third year by IRDA. If the application is rejected, TPA is not entitled to apply again within two years. The TPA should furnish all documents including the agreement with the insurance company while applying for licence. This agreement should contain details of the remuneration that may be payable to the TPA by the insurance company.

- The TPA will be allowed to enter into an agreement with more than one insurer, and similarly insurance companies can engage more than one TPA.
- The TPA has to spell out the scope of services that it will deliver, while entering into an agreement with a insurance company.
- TPAs shall not charge any fee from the clients
- IRDA guidelines do not permit marketing of health insurance policies by the TPA.
- TPAs would also have to maintain and report to IRDA on transactions carried out on behalf of the insurer. The authority expects TPAs to maintain all records properly and maintain professional confidentiality between the parties. The authority holds the power to monitor and check the performance of TPAs from time to time. TPAs are expected to furnish to the insurance company and the authority an annual report and any other return as may be required by the authority.
- IRDA has drawn up a code of conduct for the TPAs, refraining them from trading in information, submitting wrong information to insurers, and making advertisements without prior approval of the insurer, among other things. Their licence will be revoked under such instances.

IRDA regulations place stringent conditions for licensing TPAs Current regulation requires TPAs to meet a minimum equity capital of Rs 10 million. The capital requirements for entering into this sector are not stringent. As a result, there may be a proliferation of players, not all of the best quality. A large number of players will mean pressure on margins. Besides this, TPAs need to set up infrastructure which would involve large investments, the payback period of which is likely to be long. TPAs face high operating risk of obtaining economics of scale necessary to break even. Volumes are critical because the revenue generation of TPAs is linked to the number of policies they undertake to administer. According to current regulations. TPAs will get 6 per cent of the premium collected as their share of revenue.

It is expected that with the introduction of TPA services, the claim settlement process would be simplified. IRDA has suggested that all claims should be settled in seven days. In a case study done in Ahmedabad. It was observed that the insurance company takes on average 121 days to settle a claim [Bhat and Reuben 2002]. Outsourcing claim processing services may help in reducing the claim period. But settling claims in seven days is still a very ambitious target in the current scenario. TPAs will face major challenges in bringing down the settlement period to seven days. It has been observed that lack of proper documents related to treatment often results in deferred or non-payment of claims. Of course, examination of exclusion clauses in the policy is imperative before authorising admissibility and further treatment. TPAs will have to sort out these issues when the policy-holder is seeking healthcare services. Winning the confidence of policyholders and maintaining the client base will be challenging. Competitive marketing strategies and use of innovative mechanisms will be important. All attempts by insurance companies to tie up with private hospitals through the TPA system in the past have had little success, as there is generally a mutual feeling of distrust. This will pose a major challenge.

Consumer Concerns

Increased costs for consumer: Introduction of TPA services will result in higher costs. Who bears this cost? So far, government-run insurance companies were following the policy of referring claims cases to a panel of doctors. In 46 per cent cases medical referral was sought [Bhat and Reuben 20021. Insurance companies spent less than Rs 150 per case. The introduction of TPAs will have significant implications for costs. The policyholder has to bear the cost of payment to the TPA and this increase in cost will result in an increase in premium rate.

Premium of Mediclaim insurance policies has already gone up by 6 per cent. Choice of service provider: The advantage of having a TPA will certainly increase accessibility to healthcare and cashless hospitalisation facility, which did not exist in the previous system. But though patients are free to choose any hospital, for a cashless facility they may be required to go to a facility chosen by the TPA.

The delicate balance between the insurance company, providers and customers is difficult to maintain. TPAs are bound to face a number of challenges: serious pressure from insurance companies to keep the claim ratio down, lesser role in containing costs, and serious conflicts with healthcare service providers. For example, introduction of similar services in Hong Kong resulted in all local physicians deciding not to participate in the network mechanism and this seriously affected the availability of healthcare services to policyholders who were in need of treatment [Parekh 2003].

According to IRDA guidelines, TPAs are not allowed to market health insurance policies, which will result in a conflict of interest between the insurance company and the TPA on one hand and between the TPA and policyholder on the other. The system may create perverse incentives which give opportunities to healthcare providers, policyholders, and TPAs to collude, and TPAs may favour healthcare providers and policyholders in settling claims in order to attract more business. However, TPAs feel that by not allowing them to market insurance products, the health insurance sector will see less participation of TPAs in areas such as consumer education and creating awareness about various policy options, which will discourage competition in the insurance sector. As a result, the objectives of insurance reform will not be achieved.

Training of TPAS

TPA is a complex Organization and, therefore, must have a range of management competencies and capabilities which can handle sensitive customer service requirements, hardcore financial management, specialty technical/medical knowledge, and robust information technology. TPAs must be organized with an emphasis on the selection of adequately qualified personnel and an intensive comprehensive training regime [Parekh 2003].

There is no knowledge base and recognised training facilities that guide policy-makers.

Characteristics of Healthcare Provision: Quality of healthcare is a critical issue in an unregulated private medical sector [Bhat 1999]. TPAs are expected to develop a network of healthcare providers by following certain criteria such as minimum qualification of service provider and evidence that service providers follow basic minimum standards of care. However, TPAs will face a number of challenges. The minimum standards of care are not defined, healthcare service providers have a much higher bargaining power in the system and will not be persuader follow standards and quality guidelines. In many situations increased use of resources generally has no significant impact either on overall quality of care and/or health outcomes. Without proper regulation of private practice on what is being provided and at what cost, an indemnity system will continue to lead to more expensive healthcare. TPAs and IRDA will have a less influential role in regulating healthcare service providers.

Lack of standardisation or accreditation system for hospitals also causes concern over pricing and billing. Billing systems differ from facility to facility. Most of the payments are cash based and less transparent. TPAs would face difficulties in scrutinizing and processing claims and reimbursements using common standards across facilities.

There is no standardisation of charges across hospitals in the country. In many situations, billing systems are not at par with standards of care. One observes significant variations in charges across hospitals. Table 4 presents information from 670 claims and reimbursement data for various healthcare services.

One of the ways in which a managed care Organization bargains for better prices and discounts is by providing volume business. In indemnity insurance arrangement, TPAs cannot assure a certain volume of business to a particular healthcare service provider upfront. Since the insurance company and TPAs function as separate entities and the latter have to deal with a large number of service providers, offering a bulk deal to one single provider is not possible. This would have implications for the costs of medical services.

IRDA recognises that future health insurance products should be customised focusing on clients demands. There has been no actuarial involvement in designing health insurance products. A past experience is important in calculating premiums.

Table 4: Charges for Healthcare Services

Health	*Treatment Cost Range (Rs)*	*Age Group*
Enteric fever	1800-18000	5 yrs-35 yrs
Cataract	5500-20000	5 yrs-35 yrs
Gastroenteritis	1500-11000	44 yrs-66 yrs
Accidents	2000-1.71 lakh	35 yrs-50 yrs
Heart disease/chest pain	5000-1.70 lakh	35 yrs-68 yrs
Appendicitis	12000-20000	below 50

A centralised database containing information on the costs of insurers and Healthcare providers is, therefore, desirable. However, there is lack of information on healthcare services and utilization. Recognising this as a problem, IRDA has constituted a committee with representation from insurers, TPAs, the tariff advisory committee (TAG) and IRDA to suggest a framework for the collection of health-related data and advise on the use of this information in (a) building health insurance products by insurance companies, (b) establishing benchmarks for the services to be provided by TPAs, and (c) standardising the services to be provided by hospitals to policyholders [*IRDA Journal* 2003].

There is very little information and documentation on approaches that can be used to influence consumer behaviour, provider practices and restructuring the market, in both health and insurance. Approaches such as standardisation of treatment protocols as proposed by IRDA can be problematic. These efforts may imply proposing treatment practices that may be contrary to existing practices, and the regulators may face serious opposition from powerful professional groups. The monitoring function is vital but difficult to sustain in the long term. Such efforts are highly resource intensive, especially when they involve working with a large number of geographically dispersed and small-sized service providers having the backing of highly politicised professional bodies. The regulator has to make careful judgments in developing appropriate strategies to deal with private healthcare service providers.

It is also not clear how standards of care can be set without involving the service providers. Also, given the diversity of providers and absence of uniform standards, getting information on disease management and costs/pricing are going to be challenging tasks.

Other Inherent Risks and Issues

Do TPAs have an incentive in controlling costs? The remuneration of the TPA has been decided as a fixed percentage of the policy premium. In case reimbursements are controllable (which in practice they are), the payments to TPA for their services are not linked to the effort of controlling reimbursements. Hence, how TPAs are paid for their services should take into account the TPA's efforts and successes in controlling costs and reimbursements. In any insurance system, focus on prevention and promotive services can cut down many costs. TPAs can play an important role in these areas. However, the mechanisms for these are not in place and their role is not clearly defined. TPAs are in a position to offer and organise these services, but this will come at a cost.

In many situations, policyholders are not aware of various conditions and exclusion clauses in insurance policies. As a result, disputes between policyholders and insurance companies have increased and both parties have resorted to litigation. Problems arise because of lack of information and awareness, as also inadequate understanding of various nuances of insurance. It is expected that TPAs can play an important role in educating consumers and creating awareness. TPAs are the interface between the insurer and the insured and they are in a position to educate the insurer on health insurance.

TPAs point out that if they can collect money from the customer, it will mean more competition and thus better service.

On the demand-side, one positive impact of TPAs existence would be on service utilization. In most situations utilization of high cost speciality care will need approval and concurrence from the TPA. Utilization of such services would be rationed by restricting direct access to specialists. TPAs face serious challenge in mitigating the negative consequences of health insurance and control malpractices. While dealing with a large number of policyholders TPAs would be in a position to generate lot of comparable data on utilization of services and their cost structures. This information can be used to set benchmarks for costs and quality of care. However, this is going to take time. Developing these benchmarks and putting them in place will need research on understanding of cost drivers.

In order to mitigate the risks of working capital, insurance companies may be required to keep cash balances with TPAs to meet the reimbursement pressure. There is no regulation on cash management practices of TPAs. Insurance companies and IRDA need to address this area as there are perverse motives to use these funds for purposes other than meeting working capital requirements.

IRDA can revoke the TPA's licence if the latter's financial condition deteriorates at any point of time. TPAs stand as guarantor between insurer and provider of service. The risks are high. What happens if a TPA fails? Who stands as the guarantor for the TPA to meet its liabilities in case of failure? Many healthcare providers are reluctant to offer cash-less service without receiving advance from TPA. Healthcare facilities consider the risks are too high in dealing with TPAs.

IRDA has made it mandatory for health insurance companies to have significant presence in rural areas. As part of fulfilling this obligation, IRDA requires a detailed plan on how the insurance company will cover rural areas. For this, insurance companies would require TPAs to set up infrastructure in rural areas. Addressing the rural segment will be a challenge for TPAs.

There are several other areas which have not been addressed clearly in the current regulations. For example, in case there is a dispute between the TPA and insurance company, what will be the process of resolving the conflict? Who will audit TPAs? It has become mandatory for the insurance company to appoint a TPA. What will be the process of selection of the TPA? How are TPAs going to market their services? Who would set prices for TPA services'? As TPA is a new concept, there is little awareness among the people about these services provided by TPAs.

2

Third Party Administrators: Theory and Practice

There is considerable confusion on the role and usefulness of third Party administrators (TPAs) in India. The Insurance Regulatory and Development Authority (IRDA) defines TPA as 'an insurance intermediary licensed by the Authority who, either directly or indirectly, solicits or effects coverage of, underwrite, collect, charge premium from an insured, or adjust or settle claims in connection with health insurance, except as an agent or broker or an insurer.' Basically, a TPA acts as a service integrator between the insurer, the insured and the health service provider.

To provide a brief background, the Insurance Regulatory and Development Bill, which was passed by parliament in January 2000, allowed the insurance sector to open up to private players. IRDA is the apex body that will ensure that the insurance sector operates in a manner that is consistent with interest of consumers. The General Insurance Company was converted into

India's national re-insurer in December 2000, and all the subsidiaries working under the GIC umbrella were restructured as independent insurance companies. Parliament cleared a bill on July 30, IJ2002 de linking the four subsidiaries from GIC. A separate bill has been approved to allow brokers, cooperatives and intermediaries in the sector.

The TPAs were introduced as intermediaries to facilitate claims settlements between the insurer and the insured. Insurance companies have been searching for ways and means to get their management expenses in line with the specifications laid down by IRDA. Insurers can now outsource their administrative activities, including settlement of claims, to TPAs, who offer such services at a cost. Since the TPAs are paid by the insurers, it is argued that the policy holders should welcome such a move since they receive enhanced facilities at no extra cost. The other benefit of TPAs is that once the policy has been issued, the insurance companies have to pass on all the records to the TPA, and all the information regarding the insured will remain with the TPA. Finally, the new system is supposed to be based on a cashless mode, which is definitely an improvement over the previous system as far as consumers are concerned.

Ultimately, of course, the role of TPAs in the country has to be measured against the basic parameters of a functional health sector, that is, are the TPAs able to make healthcare more accessible and available to the population at large?

This paper is an attempt to understand the role of TPAs in theory and practice in India. Its findings and conclusions are based on a series of meetings, discussions and interviews with various TPAs, insurance companies and providers, and are the authors' own views. For the sake of confidentiality, names of individuals and Organizations have not been mentioned here.

Before IRDA allowed the TPAs to formally enter the market, there were intermediaries who were acting on behalf of the corporates and playing a very similar role to that of present-day TPAs. Corporates were utilising these agencies to help them make the process of claim reimbursement easier and smoother for their employees. Also, these agencies were helping to market the insurance products available mainly Mediclaim—to corporates.

The IRDA mandated that only an Organization registered under the Companies Act, 1956 with a share capital of at least Rs 1 crore could set up a TPA. Further, a minimum of Rs 1 crore worth of working capital is also mandated by the IRDA regulations.

At the time of inviting applications, it is learnt, the IRDA called a meeting of 108 potential players. With the limit of Rs 1 crore capital, only 23 TPAs remained and got registered. Of these, the Mediclaim business of the public sector insurance companies was allocated among 11 TPAs, but according to some of the TPAs contacted for this research, this list was apparently very different from the one initially drawn up by experts and other selected invitees. The initial misallocation of the Mediclaim business the reasons for which seem to be not based on any objective criteria is still seen as a major reason for the subsequent outcome in the market for Mediclaim business, which will be discussed below. It may be mentioned here that most of the health insurance business comes from the four public sector companies; the private companies at present have only about 6 per cent of the medical insurance business, and have given the business to only a couple of TPAs, The following steps are involved from the time of the policy-holder informing the TPA to the latter settling the claims.

- All the records of medical insurance policies of an insurer will be transferred to the TPA once the insurance company has given the business to a TPA.
- The TPA will issue identity cards to all policyholders. Which they have to show to the hospital authorities before availing any hospitalisation services.
- In case of a claim, policyholder has to inform the TPA on a 24-hour toll-free line provided by the latter.
- On informing the TPA, policyholder will be directed to a hospital where the TPA has a tied up arrangement. However, the policy-holder will have the option to join any other hospital of their choice, but in such case payment shall be on reimbursement basis.
- TPA issues an authorisation letter to the hospital for treatment, and will pay for the treatment.
- TPA will track the case of the insured at the hospital and at the point of discharge, all the bills will be sent to TPA.
- TPA makes the payment to the hospital.
- TPA sends all the documents necessary for consideration of claims, along with bills to the insurer.
- Insurer reimburses the TPA.

Market for TPAs in India

Health insurance premiums in India have risen from Rs 531 crore in 2000-01 to Rs 1,045 crore in 2002-03, which includes overseas medical policies (*IRDA Journal* 2003). The four public sector insurance companies have hiked premium by 6 per cent since January 2003, apparently to factor in cost escalation as a result of the appointment of TPAs as mandated by IRDA. However, this revision comes on the heels of another hefty hike of 15 per cent implemented exactly a year earlier (Business Line, December 31, 2002). The TPAs are being paid 5.5 per cent of gross premium as commission. Based on a figure of over Rs 1,000 crore of premiums, this means that the total business for TPAs in India is about Rs 50 crore. Some business is, however, being conducted without TPAs. Based on the rate of growth of insurance premiums in just one year, it is possible that health insurance will grow much more in coming years, giving more business to the TPAs.

Given the current business of about Rs 50 crore, it may seem that even these 23 TPAs are probably too many. The market is already divided among some that have cornered the major part of the business. However, while bigger TPAs are more effective, for pan-Indian operations, some of the smaller TPAs are also doing well in terms of quality of service, in their limited areas of operation. Success or lack of it depends on a fine balance of essentially three parameters: (a) share of total business, (b) availability of capital, and (c) geographic spread of operations. As in any market, the unsuccessful players are expected to exit the business. In the TPA market, the inefficient players, who are not able to satisfy their main customers, would in theory exit the market; however, as will be discussed below, this has not really happened in India. The reason ultimately is that the TPA market is not really like any other market: neither the entry nor the exit of TPAs from the market is really free. As mentioned above, the entry of TPAs was based on rationing of the total business and not a natural entry based on market considerations. Similarly, the exit of inefficient TPAs is also not due to market forces and, in fact, has not taken place at all.

As mentioned earlier, one of the main benefits of a TPA to the customer is a cashless transaction at the time of service delivery. Clearly, this mode of business requires the TPAs to have sufficient working capital to make payments to the hospital. Given the cashless system of settlements being encouraged under the Mediclaim scheme, insurance companies are insisting on bank guarantees from TPAs.

To illustrate how the system works, let us assume that the claims ratio of Mediclaim is 100 per cent. This means that for a premium of Rs 1 crore (Rs 100 lakh) per annum, the claim would also be Rs 100 lakh. Let us also assume that the turnaround time -the time taken from the time of service delivery to the payment by the insurance company to the TPA—for a claim on average is 15 days (presuming efficient turnaround time). For a 15-day period, the claim amount would be around Rs 4 lakh on an annual claim of Rs 100 lakh. Hence if the insurance company insists on bank guarantees, and the turnaround time for claims is on average 15 days, then for each Rs 1 crore of business, the TPA has to arrange for a bank guarantee of Rs 4 lakh. The bank would charge a commission while issuing the bank guarantee. Further, it would also insist on a cash margin. If the margin requirement were 50 per cent of the bank guarantee, then Rs 2. lakh cash margin would have to be provided for the issuance of a bank guarantee of Rs 4 lakh for business worth Rs. 1 crore. For business worth Rs. 1,000 crore, bank guarantees worth Rs. 40 crore would have to be provided. This would require a cash margin of Rs. 20 crore, assuming 50 per cent margin. Thus the requirement of working capital for TPAs goes up substantially. This example clearly indicates that pan-Indian operations would require a substantial amount of working capital for TPAs and of bank guarantee in proportion to the size of the business. Initially, some TPAs could not make the reimbursements to the hospitals and/or the customers on time, with resultant confusion and frustration on the part of all the stakeholders. Even now, some hospitals continue to complain about not receiving payment on time.

As for the basic design of the new system of cashless payment, it is clear that the entire system is not as yet cashless; a significant portion of the Mediclaim business is still in the form of reimbursement to the policyholder. One TPA mentioned a 30-70 split between cashless and reimbursement; however, this may vary widely among TPAs. The reason for not moving over to the cashless system could be both a preference of consumers who like to visit their selected hospitals that are not on the TPA network, or the hospitals, who prefer to be paid by patients directly rather than wait for settlement. A third reason is an emergency situation where the consumer does not have much of a choice.

Benefits of TPAS—Theoretical

With the Indian healthcare scenario of high out-of-pocket payment for curative care—both hospital and domiciliary, limited health insurance for the majority of the population, uncontrolled expansion of the private health sector and falling standards of government healthcare facility, there is understandably a lot of confusion about what should be the ideal set of reforms. However, it was clear that the health insurance sector illnesses. It was also quite obvious that the four public sector general insurance companies were unable to offer a product that was more useful or consumer-friendly than Mediclaim as it was designed in the beginning. Finally, the reimbursement process for even those few who had the policy was arduous and complicated enough to diminish the value of the benefits considerably in the eyes of the customer.

In this scenario, privatisation of the insurance sector and the subsequent creation of the system of TPAs meant that there was a possibility of more efficiency in the insurance market because of more competition as well as the creation of a professional cadre to look after Speedy disposal of payments. Thus, outsourcing of the service facility did make eminent sense, especially given the service quality of PSU companies. Average time for claim processing before the TPAs came into existence was apparently much longer than what it is now: some TPAs claim that the settlement is done in a matter of days. Due to lack of adequate data, it is not really clear what the current average turnaround time is.

Secondly, the cashless system is definitely an improvement over the reimbursement scheme, and the choice set for such cashless transactions expanded when the TPAs succeeded in enlisting many more hospitals and nursing homes on the approved list eligible for cashless facility.

From the perspective of the insurance companies, the TPAs benefit them by bringing down the claims ratio, by reducing false claims as well as standardising treatment costs. While the standardisation has still not been completed, if it happens it would benefit the consumers immensely, at least in theory. It appears that the incurred claims ratio of. PSU companies in health insurance has been brought down to 91.07 per cent in 2002-03 from 99.21 per cent in 2001-02 [Gupta 2003]. How much of this improvement is on account of TPAs is, of course, a point that needs more analysis.

Finally, the TPAs can play a huge role in making appropriate data available for actuarial calculations, because they are the recipients of morbidity data that are linked with individual characteristics such as age. From a research and policy perspective too, the availability of such data is of immense value.

Experience With TPAS

The initial performance of TPAs has not been up to the mark, for several reasons, one of the main being the inability of some of them to deliver the goods. Perhaps the best way to introduce the TPAs was to run a pilot scheme and iron out teething problems, instead of changing the system almost overnight that involved a different mode of functioning for all the stakeholders. With so many TPAs entering the market with different capabilities and capital, it is not surprising that much confusion ensued. Those that had good links with hospitals earlier or who invested in tying up technologically with hospitals seem to be doing better than others. Similarly, TPAs that had not spread out too fast and too thinly across India seemed to have performed better than others. Unfortunately, discussions with insurance companies indicated that despite their non-performance, the TPAs were not blacklisted due to non-professional considerations.

There are some other features of the new system that need to be taken into account to evaluate the functioning and usefulness of TPAs.

Individual vs corporate business: Firstly, there is no doubt that the individual health insurance business is cross-subsidising corporate business (often known as accommodation business). The informal nexus among corporate houses, corporate hospitals, insurance companies and TPAs is ensuring that the claims ratio is high on corporate insurance, and low on individual insurance. Insurance companies agreed off the record that there often is pressure from corporate houses on insurance companies to get specific claims settled. This obviously means that ordinary policyholders are being subjected to stricter scrutiny. Incentive for hospitals: For hospitals that are not also offering TPA or insurance services, there does not seem to be a great incentive to move over to the TPA system with delayed payment in contrast to the earlier system of on-the-spot payment. The discussions did indicate that some hospitals were not getting their payments on time and were reluctant to work with some of the current TPAs. However, as more and more health insurance policies are issued, even leading hospitals have to deal with TPAs. On the other side, some TPAs were of the opinion that the hospitals do not send the requisite information to them in time for them to be able to process the claims. The view is that hospitals have to be given substantial training before they can actually be an efficient part of this new system.

However, discussions with hospitals revealed that demand for hospital care has been increasing substantially with the new TPA system, and that it is in the hospitals interests to move over to the TPA system. Nevertheless, it probably continues to be true that demand for insurance-linked hospital care is mostly centred around the upper end of the tertiary care sector, with more expensive and super specialty hospitals benefiting the most from the new system. Hospital-backed TPAs: there is already evidence that a couple of hospital chains have got TPA licence. This is certainly unethical and against the basic guidelines laid down by IRDA. This system will ensure that the TPA/hospital will work towards its own system, and there is always a possibility of playing favourites, that is, smooth claim settlement towards this hospital, and not to the other hospitals. This kind of system is, therefore, likely to bring in malpractices. Similarly, there are instances where insurance brokers have also ventured into the TPA business through a sister concern. There are implications of conflict of interest in this situation. At present, TPAs are not allowed to market health insurance policies due to a conflict of interest. However, it cannot be denied that a TPA that sells the policy will probably have an incentive to offer better services. Legally, it is difficult not to allow promoters to enter allied businesses as suitable equity structuring can always be done. But, due to the possibility of unethical practices, the IRDA/ insurance companies need to ensure that a strict separation is maintained between these businesses.

There are also instances of some TPAs working on behalf of corporates (*IRDA Journal,* January 2003), which is another area of collusion that is fraught with inefficient outcomes. In fact, a notice from the IRDA to TPAs and general insurers says that "it has been observed of late by the authority that the offices of various insurance companies and licensed third party administrators—health services are entering into agreements at the insistence of their clients for the sake of business considerations allowing TPAs to charge separate fees in addition to insurance premium. These TPAs although licensed by the authority, perforce have to enter into such agreements to ensure the survival of their operations in view of the reluctance by insurance companies to empanel and utilise them. It is hereby clarified that in the case of all such agreements which are out of the scope of IRDA (Third Party Administrators - Health Services) Regulations, 2001 adequate precautions must be taken by informing the customer clearly of this fact." While it is not clear exactly what this entails and how and what the customer should be informed about, the recognition of this phenomenon is an important development within IRDA.

These points indicate that the system of TPAs, while theoretically sound and useful, is in practice fraught with problems. The first issue is that different TPAs face different constraints in terms of capital, capacity and connections. This immediately implies that it is not a level playing field for the functioning of the TPAs. Therefore, there is an incentive among the stakeholders 10 form liaisons and collude. Almost all the stakeholders, except the policyholders, have a business angle. Given that the total market is limited, each one is trying to grab a major share. Among the TPAs, some hold a major share of the total business, while the smaller players are trying to stay afloat. One sure way of ensuring a greater share of the insurance market, administration of insurance and hospital services is by collusions and mergers, a natural phenomenon of imperfect markets. One method of collusion is informal payment or bribes. Corruption has been mentioned by everyone with whom discussions were held, clearly indicating that the TPA is not functioning as a competitive system with efficient outcomes. Corruption or non-market methods of allocation of business result in distortions and unnecessary system. Costs, which are then passed on to consumers as higher prices or premiums. Ultimately, in such a system, the policyholders have the most to lose.

Cost to Consumer: customers are paying for the extra service being provided by TPAs through a higher premium. If, in fact, the claims ratio is coming down and the insurance companies are being freed of their workload, then the savings in terms of both money and other administrative costs should be passed on to the consumers. This is currently not happening; insurance companies are not passing on the savings made in outsourcing administrative work being done by the TPAs. Of course, the claims ratio may be not coming down as significantly as it seems due to the presence of family floaters that are now being offered by insurance companies.

Marketing the Universal Health Scheme: A new finance ministry initiative has been the universal health scheme, which was targeted at the poor. The premium of Re 1 per day was designed to bring in large sections of the less-well-to-do population under the insurance net. This has not happened for a variety of reasons, one of the most important being that poor families find it hard to pay Rs. 365 per person or Rs. 548 for a family per annum. Another reason for this scheme not doing well has been the lack of marketability of the product and the difficulty of reaching populations in the rural areas. The margin of profits for TPAs in this business is very low, and the TPAs do not seem to be interested in raising their share of this product. The insurance companies also do not seem to be very aggressive about selling this product to those below the poverty line, only 3,576 families of the 2,50,000 families covered were below the poverty line. The relevance of this in the context of the TPAs lies in scaling up of insurance for communities that are hard to reach or which are not apparently profitable to the companies. Given the low educational and economic status of communities that do not really understand insurance procedures, the role of TPAs takes on even greater significance. But the incentives are not conducive for them to want to service these policyholders.

Cost of Healthcare: Cashless facility increases the capacity of policyholders to incur higher costs at the time of illness, and therefore has a tendency to inflate the demand for high-cost care. This could be limited to a certain extent with the presence of a system of co-payments. In any case, this tendency will be reinforced from the supply side, and there is a real fear that the presence of TPAs will facilitate the inherent cost-increasing nature of the current system, resulting in welfare loss for consumers. The mechanism is as follows: the presence of insurance will result in supplier-induced demand especially in diagnostics and super-specialty treatment. Hospitals would like to shape up for these types of services, which can only be done by accruing additional revenues from higher prices of healthcare. In principle, it is conceivable that: *(a)* consumers who do not have insurance pay higher costs, *(b)* consumers who do not have access to such five-star hospitals also pay the same high premiums, and *(c)* every policyholder may end up paying higher premiums sooner or later, that is, insurance companies may clamour for revision of premiums in the near future. Some of this could be limited if the insurance policies are more flexible in terms of the kind of facilities that can be availed: for instance, with sub-limits, those who pay more can avail of costlier facilities. Of course, with more extensive coverage, and a certain degree of standardisation of services/ costs, the increase in premiums can be contained somewhat.

The other reason why premiums may go up would be the inability of TPAs to make enough profits, especially those TPAs that are spread out all over the country. Discussions with many TPAs revealed that there is dissatisfaction with the 5.5 percent commission. There is a lot of variation in calculating break-even among the TPAs on account of their in-built costs. One player estimated the break-even in metros at Rs 10 crore of premium business and for non-metros at Rs 4 crore, while another estimated the break-even premium at Rs 100 crore for the TPA. Some TPAs frankly admitted that they were making losses as of now, and hoped to turn things around in a few more years. The public: sector general insurance companies should be bringing down their total management costs from about 30 per cent to about 20 per cent (as per the Insurance Act).

Do insurance companies have any incentive to control the systemic costs? No. Since corporate clients are keeping the bulk of the business afloat, and also because of the influence they have with insurance companies, their claims are seldom rejected, though some TPAs argue that corporate claims have gone down because they have been able to reject wrong claims. Cost control, is not something that they are consciously seeking to do. The TPAs—by turning around payments quickly will only add to these tendencies of higher prices of healthcare; higher the turnover of patients, greater the incentive for hospitals to make higher per-unit profits.

Thus, while it is too early to say much yet, there is some reason to believe that the system has no in-built mechanism for cost control, and none of the important players seems to be worried about this aspect. The lack of a mechanism for cost control has been mentioned by others [Bhat 2003] and will likely remain an important issue for sometime.

Role of IRDA

The discussion so far indicates that the system of TPAs can work if one tries and avoids the pitfalls. And since regulation and development were the two key functions of the IRDA, it has to play these two roles, instead of letting things take their own course. We list out below some of the areas that need greater attention by the IRDA.

- IRDA could attempt to amend current regulations so that some of the sources of malpractice could be stemmed. For instance, the practice of hospital-backed TPAs is likely to give rise to conflict of interests, which can be taken care of by a right set of regulations.
- It must review the performance of each TPA objectively, especially with regard to unethical practices.

- How many TPAs is an optimum number at this juncture? This question needs to be looked at by the IRDA, together with the insurance companies and the TPAs. If necessary, a revision of the list may be undertaken in an objective fashion.
- Review the role of TPA. Should the TPAs be allowed to market health insurance products? Would that be a more transparent system than the one currently in operation,, where side deals seem j to be going on, especially since the market is not large enough; for everyone.
- One of the main reasons for opening up the sector was to encourage health insurance. That does not seem to be happening; despite the need for it. Allowing individual policyholders to subsidise corporate policyholders goes counter to this line of thinking, and IRDA must intervene to prevent this from happening,
- If private players have been provided insurance licences on the basis of business plans that include health insurance, then IRDA must ensure that the health insurance business plans be Implemented and not just remain on paper. IRD A could also think in terms of the approach adopted in the case of rural/social sector insurance businesses, wherein minimum business targets have to be achieved. Private players with foreign partners should be encouraged to introduce innovative health insurance plans they already run in other countries.
- Currently, the requirement of paid up capital of Rs. 100 crore is a huge barrier to entry for health

insurance companies in India. IRDA must review this provision at the earliest, if it wants the business to expand.

- IRDA needs to conduct studies, with external expertise if required, on various aspects of TPAs functioning. On a continuing basis, external auditors need to check on various aspects of health insurance as is being conducted by insurance companies and TPAs. External auditors can also check on any nexus that may develop among TPAs, service providers, corporates and insurance companies.
- Individual policyholders need the support of the regulator as well as the government departments like the health and finance ministries. The insurance ombudsman can play an important role once there is a specific complaint, but the regulator needs to study the aspects of functioning of the entire health insurance operation in order to improve matters.
- Finally, many TPAs mentioned their eagerness to turn themselves into more evolved players like HMOs/health insurance companies after they acquire sufficient knowledge and expertise. Already, a few have started innovating and providing health management services. IRDA needs to give this possibility some serious thought along with other health sector experts, to understand the ramifications of such a system in terms of equity and efficiency of healthcare delivery.

Role of Health Ministry

While the IRDA is supposed to regulate the entire insurance market, it remains the task of the ministry of health and family welfare to oversee the functioning of the healthcare market. There are certain chores for the ministry to attend to.

- Firstly, it must revisit the issue of separating health insurance from other non-health products [Ellis et al 2000, Mahal 2000], due to the social welfare aspects of health. While risk pooling is ideally done across different markets, within the health insurance sector there is enough heterogeneity to ensure adequate risk pooling. Once this is done, the parameters of evaluating the performance of both insurance companies and TPAs can be set against the backdrop of an equitable and efficient health market.
- Accreditation of healthcare providers has been talked about for a long time, much before TPAs arrived on the scene [Nandraj and Khot 2003], and remains a stumbling block in ensuring a functioning healthcare market in India. The ministry must take the lead in ensuring that this happens at the earliest, so that consumers are better able to understand the quality of services availed.
- Similarly, standardisation of services with ratings is important in the context of insurance and TPAs. This again is an area where the ministry has to play a lead role.
- The finance ministry and health ministry need to work closely more together on health insurance products. The fact that the universal health

scheme was born in the finance ministry and has not really taken off gives cause for concern. Formulating workable health insurance schemes for the poor is a long drawn-out effort as it will involve data and research in several areas, such as needs assessment, type of healthcare to be offered under insurance, proper costing, arriving at insurance premium based on the ability to pay, identifying the element of subsidy involved, distribution of the product to the identified population, educating the targeted population, and identifying service providers. Clearly, this needs the attention of different ministries, with the health ministry taking the lead. A pilot scheme is the way to begin, after involving various stakeholders. The ministry of health can and should play a much more proactive role in formulating appropriate products for the targeted population.

- The ministry of health and family welfare came out with a report in 2003 the health insurance market, which is worth mentioning here. Among other recommendations, the committee stressed that the government should:

(1) Introduce rating and credentialing of the providers; *(2)* Create common standards and norms for coding of diseases and treatment procedures; *(3)* Adopt standard health codes; *(4)* Create an information bank on insurance, diseases and treatment; *(5)* Ensure portability across players and schemes.

These recommendations remain valid in the context of this discussion.

The IRDA and the ministry of health should jointly ensure that the TPAs play an active role in community health insurance schemes as well as the universal health scheme. The need for cashless facilities for communities is more significant than corporate or ordinary households, but there is as yet only a limited use of TPAs in such schemes.

In sum, it can be safely said that TPAs can potentially play an important role in making insured healthcare availability smoother, but it cannot be seen as a panacea for all the problems of the health sector, nor can it be blamed for these problems. The functioning of the TPA is limited, but if not regulated and checked, there is some danger that consumer interests may not be as safe under this system as one would wish.

3

Recent Welfare Schemes: An Assessment

The social sector is ever the Cinderella of the government family—always there in the background, but never the centre of anyone's attention. For all political personalities there is a professional compulsion to hype up their commitment to the basic human needs and rights of their constituents. It is the type of subject that generates a gushing rhetoric wrapped in the most empathetic language. However, when it comes to taking initiative, the functionaries, whether political or bureaucratic, are easily distracted. India, even in its brashly globalised incarnation, is still a developing country, desperately scrambling around for fulfilling its basic human needs. Yet, our country is one that has virtually no social security net for most of the population. The state health network, though intended to be comprehensive, only gives a modicum of health services to whoever is fortunate enough to be able to access it—its capacity is extremely limited as a result of both inadequate resources and the indifferent attitude of the health service personnel. Outside this, the formal sector has mandatory schemes covering the risk of sickness and death, and providing provident fund and pension benefits for government and private sector employees. But, for the un organized sector there are only a few scattered non-statutory schemes with limited population coverage.

In the recent past the government has announced two new initiatives in the social sector—Universal Health Insurance Scheme (UHIS) and the Unorganized Sector Workers' Social Security Scheme (SSS)—which appear substantive by way of coverage, and merit scrutiny. Several packages of private health insurance have been available even earlier, though they are expensive and cover a tiny population. The aggregate coverage under the private health insurance schemes is less than 1.0 million. The formal sector has for long had mandatory welfare schemes, though scattered and on a relatively small scale - Central Government Health Scheme (CGHS) providing a health cover for the government employees; Central Government Employees Group Insurance Scheme providing a life cover for government employees; Employees State Insurance Scheme (ESIS) providing health and life cover for private employees; and the Employees Provident Fund and Miscellaneous Provisions Act providing different schemes for provident fund/deposit-linked insurance/pension for private employees (The Employees Provident Funds Scheme, 1952; Employees Deposit-Linked Insurance Scheme, 1976; Employees Pension Scheme, 1995). These formal sector mandatory schemes have an aggregate coverage of about 40 million. In addition to all this, the scattered employer-based schemes in the formal sector have provided varying degrees of Social security to about

30 million individuals, while community-based insurance schemes have provided some cover to 30 million people. In totality, some degree of social security cover has been. Available to about 110 million people, out of which less than 30 million are the poor from the unorganized sector. The budget of 2003-04 launched the UHIS in the country. UHIS is the first broad-based health security scheme, having an element of financial contribution from the state. This could, therefore, be said to be within the ambit of 'social health insurance.

Universal Health Insurance Scheme

This scheme, principally, offers a package of insurance cover for a limited reimbursement of expenses for hospital services. The scheme envisages reimbursement of hospitalisation expenses to an individual/family, subject to specific sub-limits relating to room/bed expenses; specialist/nursing expenses; maximum reimbursement for a single illness, etc. The aggregate quantum of cover is Rs. 30,000, subject to a sub-cap of Rs 15,000 for a single illness. The aggregate cover of Rs 30,000 can be availed of on a 'floater' basis in the case of insurance cover for a family. The scheme also provides personal accident cover of Rs 25,000 for the contingency of accidental death of the earning head of a family; and provides a disability cover, by way of a per diem compensation to an earning head of family, during his hospitalisation on account of accident/illness, for a maximum of fifteen days. The coverage under the health insurance scheme, inter alia, excludes all pre-existing diseases, as also some common medical conditions even when contracted after enrolment under the scheme. The insurance cover becomes substantively effective after the expiry of 30 days from the enrolment of the subscriber. The premium payable for this package of cover under the UHIS is Rs 365 per annum (Rs. 1 per day) for an individual; Rs 548 per annum (Rs. 1.50 per day) for a family of up to five members (including the first three children); and Rs 730 per annum (Rs. 2 per day) for a family of up to seven members (including the first three children and dependent parents). The states contribution of Rs. 100 per family comes by way of a subsidy towards the premium for BPL beneficiaries. The policy covers the expenditure incurred during hospitalisation in listed health service centres (i.e., government hospitals/nursing homes; hospitals/nursing homes registered with local authorities; and empanelled hospitals operated by NGOs/trusts/private parties, having the prescribed infrastructure facilities/qualified professional manpower). Settlement of claims under the scheme is to be carried out through TPAs/insurance companies. The scheme envisages the providing of cashless services, to the extent possible, by registering the hospitals/nursing homes. Finally, the scheme is available to groups consisting of a minimum of 100 individual/family subscribers. Some observations on the structure of the current scheme are offered hereafter.

The scheme does not seem to be based on a rigorous actuarial analysis. The prescribed premium (Rs. 365 per annum for an individual beneficiary; Rs. 110 per annum per beneficiary in a family of five; and Rs. 104 per annum per beneficiary in a family of seven), is unrealistically low. In the unorganized sector, if the household is able to afford a premium of Rs. 365 per annum for insuring the health of the head of the household, it is more than likely that it will find it good value to cover the entire family in either of the two available family variants. In these circumstances, the average premium received under the scheme would be a little above Rs. 100 per beneficiary per annum. For purposes of comparison, the only other reasonably large-span private insurance scheme existing in the country is the Mediclaim scheme of General Insurance Corporation (GIC). Here the quantum of monetary coverage under health insurance ranges from Rs 15,000 to Rs. 3,00,000 and the premium ranges from Rs 175 per annum to Rs. 5,770 per annum. The economic profile of the subscribers reveals a marked skew towards the low-income section—73 per cent subscribers belong to that category with income less than Rs. 2,500 per month. Under this scheme, the average premium paid by the subscriber was Rs. 717 per annum in the year 2000-01. The operational results of CGHS and ESIS—the mandatory schemes in the formal sector—indicate an expenditure of Rs. 203 and Rs. 313 respectively per beneficiary in the year 1999-2000. In the backdrop of the operational performance of the above-mentioned health insurance schemes, the premium proposed to be charged under the UHIS— Rs. 110 per annum (approx)—is likely to be way short of the requirement for viability. The government subsidy towards the premium is a nominal amount (Rs. 100), and that too against the subscribers contribution, only for BPL families. It needs to be recalled that in the Mediclaim scheme of GIC, the average premium collected is Rs 717 per beneficiary, and even with that, the claims: premium ratio was over 90 per cent, making it, in its present form, intrinsically nonviable. In this backdrop of practical experience, the UHIS, with its proposed premium structure would be a non-starter. To have any impact, the government subsidy would have to be substantially increased, and that too not limited only to the poorest section of the society. If the increased subsidy is limited to only the poorest section, the composition of the subscriber pool would be steeply skewed towards those with very high health risk. Such a composition would make the scheme high-cost and fundamentally non-viable. The core requirement is that government subsidise the entire insured pool equally, and that too at a much higher subsidy rate—i.e., a rate realistically linked to the actual costs of the scheme. In order to determine the realistic cost of the scheme, first a modest package of health services will have to be delineated. It must be immediately clarified that such a strategy would not result in the subsidising of the economic elite. Even if the UHIS is efficiently run, the scale and quality of services would still remain modest, and anyone who can afford it would choose to obtain superior private health services at personal cost.

Thus, there is no reason to believe that this suggestion would result in a gross misapplication of state subsidy.

The financial viability of the insurance scheme improves if the coverage is of a large representative pool of subscribers located in a compact geographical block. To some extent the UHIS adheres to this principle by placing the condition that the insurance cover will only be available to groups of at least one hundred families. A large representative group of subscribers ensures that the scheme has a balanced risk profile to make the operations cost-effective. Experience with the mediclaim scheme of GIC has shown that, out of the group that can afford to pay the premium, the response in the lower income slab is much greater. This tendency of 'adverse selection' has to be consciously countered in the UHIS. Large pools of subscribers will ensure that individuals of all economic groups are appropriately represented, so that a viable insurance scheme can be based on 'community-risk' rating rather than on 'individual risk' rating. The operation of the subscriber pool in a compact geographical block, with service delivery centres proximately located within the block, would also make it possible to create larger pools.

In order to spread this scheme in the rural areas, the service delivery centres should not be limited to hospitals and nursing homes run only by government and local authorities—the reach of the service centres will have to be increased several fold in order to stretch out to the remote areas of the country, where the quantum of unmet health needs is the highest. The insurance authorities operating the scheme will have to quickly draw up and notify the guidelines for empanelment of non-state-funded delivery centres. Also, a protocol for technical audit of theses centres would have to be expeditiously drawn up, and periodic audit will have to be conducted to screen and renew the empanelment of service centres under the insurance scheme.

The 'exclusion' provisions under the scheme are too wide in their span. If all pre-existing diseases are to be excluded, this would imply that at the time of entry, the applicant would have to be fighting fit to be eligible. It is understandable that the policy must guard against misuse—often, individuals are known to apply for the health insurance policy after observing early symptoms of a medical condition requiring serious and costly treatment. In this context, the bar to claims for illness contracted in the first thirty days of the policy is acceptable. But, for pre-existing diseases, a reasonable monetary cap can be placed on the reimbursement for certain pre-existing diseases that may require prolonged (even lifelong) treatment. The insurance scheme is most required for the poor of the unorganized sector, and the exclusion of all pre-existing diseases would effectively defeat the principal purpose of the scheme.

The scheme, as it is shaped today, only covers the risk of hospitalisation. Such schemes are known to be easier to manage. The coverage of primary health care—i.e., community health measures and ambulatory care—requires much greater skills of management and greater Organizational strength. Therefore, in the initial stage it is, perhaps, understandable that the promoters test the waters by launching schemes only covering the risk of hospitalisation. However, if the scheme is to truly become a universal health scheme, it must include in its package of services primary health care consisting of community health services and ambulatory services. Community health services promote good health through advocacy of healthy practices and reduce morbidity through preventive initiatives. Initiatives in this sector involve advocacy, sensitisation of the target population and influencing the mind-set of the citizenry. Such initiatives are low cost in character and have a long-lasting impact on the health scenario. Ambulatory care is also a very cost-effective form of health intervention. Cost studies of the primary health care services provided by NGOs over their small-span project population, have shown astonishingly low annual cost (Rs. 15 to Rs. 90), per beneficiary, with visible improvement of the principal health parameters of the beneficiary population. It is self-evident that the introduction of community health services and ambulatory care in the health cover package would reduce the burden of high cost hospitalisation. In sum, the inclusion of primary sector health care component in the UHIS would immensely increase its viability while, simultaneously providing much more useful health care services to the subscribers.

The scheme, as it exists today, is only in the nature of a preliminary statement of intent of a possible initiative. Its present form is not adequately fleshed out to successfully implement it across the entire country. It is, perhaps, because of this state of under-preparedness that the beneficiary response to the scheme has so far been negligible. Some of the key features need to be reconfigured. We need to experiment with various models of the scheme on a pilot scale. For that purpose, NGOs like SEWA, can be commissioned with state funding to carry out such studies. The different modules to be tested can be designed by varying the critical parameters, like: differing baskets of services; differing cost of each package; differing sizes of the subscriber pool; compact block vis-a-vis a scattered subscriber pool; state-funded service centres vis-a-vis private service centres; differing quantum of subscriber contribution towards and its acceptability to the subscriber; and different management agencies (i.e. voluntary Organizations like SEWA; trusts; group of wards in municipalities; PRIs-taluka panchayats/gram panchayats). Given a few years of experimentation, there is no reason to feel that it would not be possible to converge on a viable and affordable health insurance package.

Taking an overview of the UHIS, what can be said to be its main deficiencies? In order to sell itself to the finance wing of the insurance company, and to the finance ministry of the central government, the crafters of the scheme have deliberately underestimated the resource requirements. One can make the scheme more palatable by phasing it gently over a longer time span; but, under-estimating the unit cost of the insurance package would be self-defeating. Pilot studies would only be useful if they cover a reasonable package of services at a realistic cost. Underfinanced packages are bound to be a failure and would even rule out the possibility of a phased implementation in the future. In this context the government may even settle for a slower start to the scheme provided it is fully funded in the areas where it is tried out.

Social Security Scheme for Unorganized Sector

As a part of its pre-election hamper of goodies, the previous ND A government had announced the launching of pilot projects for a social security scheme for workers of the unorganized sector engaged in scheduled employments. The plan was to cover 25 lakh workers in 50 districts over the next two years under the pilot projects. The total number of workers within this sector is 367 million, constituting 93 per cent of the total number of workers employed. The ultimate objective was to enact an overarching law—the Unorganized Sector Workers Act—to regulate the employment and conditions of service of all the workers of the unorganized sector, and to provide for their safety, social security, health and welfare. The proposed legislation also sets out the conditions of service of workers in the unorganized sector. The social security scheme—the unorganized sector workers social security scheme—will ultimately operate under the umbrella of the new statute. The proposed legislation envisage the establishment of a central unorganized sector workers board, along with similar boards at the state level. The boards would, *inter alia,* advise the government on policy matters, formulate welfare schemes and review their implementation. The board would have representatives of all the stakeholders. It was also planned to set up workers' facilitation centres the implementation of the provisions of the law in different parts of the country The package of benefits offered as a part of the SSS has the following significant components:

(i) An old age pension of Rs 500 per month on attaining the age of 60 years (in the case of full and regular contribution; or other cases, it will be proportionately above or below that). Also provisions for pension to widows/orphans; *(ii)* a personal accident insurance cover of Rs 1,00,000; *(iii)* a universal health insurance scheme package for a family of five (including first three children), identical to that launched in the budget of year 2003-04 (a variant of the health cover package for three members of the family is also offered).

Under the old age pension scheme, the subscribers of the unorganized sector were to be divided into two age groups group I: age 18-35 years; group II: age 36-50 years. Enrolment under group II would be restricted to the first five years of the scheme, after which entry would only be under the group I eligibility norm. The eligibility to the benefits of the SSS will be limited to workers with wages up to Rs 6,500 per month. To participate in the integrated scheme the workers of group 1 would have to contribute Rs 50 per month and workers from group I would contribute Rs 100 per month. The scheme envisaged that the employer's contribution will be equal to that of the employee However, as is widely known, only a few individuals of the unorganized sector have steady employment. It is, therefore, very difficult in most cases to legally determine the identity of this employer. The self-employed, and such workers whose employers are not identifiable, could also register under the scheme but on payment of their contribution as also the employer contribution. As a general commitment, the scheme envisage governments own contribution of 1.16 per cent of the monthly wages of the enrolled workers, though this is in no sense related to the uncovered gap between the employer/employee contribution and the cost of the scheme. On the basis of an actuaria computation carried out by government, the cost of the old age pension component of the scheme was determined as Rs. 49 per beneficiary for group I subscribers and Rs. 1,739 per beneficiary for group II subscribers. The current plan was to increase the coverage by five million subscribers every year, reaching a ultimate target of 50 million workers over 10 years. To moderate the resulting financial burden on the government, it was propose to enroll 45 million group I subscribers and five million group II subscribers, the intake of group II subscribers being restricted only to the first five years. Since group II subscribers were can advanced age group, their need for medical services would be greater; also, their annual subscription would be collected over a shorter period before they become eligible for old age pension The assumed cost for accident insurance cover under the SS was Rs 30 per annum, while the cost for health insurance cove, was taken as Rs. 548 per annum for all subscribers. In other words the aggregate cost for the entire package of welfare benefits would be Rs. 1,071 per annum for group I workers and Rs. 2,317 annum for group II workers. The income-expenditure calculation for the above-described scheme reveals that the premium contribution will be in excess of the estimated expenditure by an aggregate amount of Rs. 5,429 crore in the first 10 years. It has been assessed that about 20 per cent of the workers who would be enrolled under the scheme, would be from the central sphere and 80 per Scent would be from the state sphere. However, the assumption of· the employer's contribution being realised from the identified employers, or in the absence of that from the subscriber, is not a realistic one. To the extent of shortfall in employer's contribution, the financial burden of meeting the deficit would then be shared roughly in the stated proportion between the centre and the states.

It would be useful to briefly discuss the financial viability of some variants of this proposed scheme. In one variant which was considered at one stage, it was assumed that the employers contribution would be double that of the enrolled employee, and that about 30 per cent of the employers would be identifiable for obtaining the employers' contribution. It was assumed that the subscribers contribution would be Rs 600 per annum in the first five years and Rs. 720 per annum thereafter. It was not envisaged that in cases where the employer could not be identified, the subscriber would have to make good the deficit contribution. In that variant, the gap between the premium contribution and the estimated expenditure would be Rs. 1,475 crore in the first five years, after which a gently rising trend of surplus is expected. In the case of this variant the net deficit is estimated to be Rs. 1,050 crore in the first

10 years of operations—the appropriate government (centre or state) would have to provide a subsidy ranging from Rs. 127 crore in the first year to Rs. 421 crore in the fifth year, before the scheme breaks even. However, this variant—assuming a contribution of the employer at twice that of the employee—is unrealistic, and now appears to have been abandoned. In yet a third variant of the scheme, equal subscription by the employee and employer at the rate of Rs. 365 per annum (i.e., Rs. 1 per day) was envisaged. Needless to say, this variant would be even more financially precarious than the other variant described above.

It is apparent that the proposed SSS is an extremely complex one, which requires a well-structured administrative framework. Some of the essential features which are needed to be put in place through the administrative framework are: efficient network for enrolment of workers and collection of the premium, if necessary (in more than one installment; a simple and workable procedure for identification of the employers and for collection of their contribution; an administrative system and an appropriate set of procedures for the disbursement of pension under the old age pension scheme; a procedure for processing the disability claims under the scheme; guidelines for empanelling the service delivery centres (hospitals/ nursing homes) for providing services; firming up of a protocol for technical audit of the service providing centres; and a system for quick processing of reimbursement claims under the health insurance scheme. The administrative cost of running the scheme has currently been projected as 1 per cent. The scheme envisages that at the central level it will be coordinated and supervised by the existing Organization—Employees

Provident Fund Organization—through its offices in different parts of the country. State governments offices and the local self-government institutions will also be engaged in the supervision and management of the scheme. At this point of time here does not appear to be enough robust field data to immediately formulate operational guidelines to implement the SSS in a countrywide scale. Therefore, the outline of the scheme, it this juncture, can only be called a work in progress. In these circumstances it was considered prudent by government to carry out pilot studies in a variety of operational settings before freezing the contours of a viable social security package for implementation over the entire country. The SSS, if it, is to expand extensively, will have to be implemented by several categories of agencies. Non-profit Organizations (NGOs, trusts, faith-based Organizations) have a considerable presence in the arena of social welfare, through their scattered programmes of varying sizes. The government plans to implement the proposed SSS through any suitable implementing agency available.

The proposed SSS is a long Over due initiative to take some substantive measures for the welfare of the workers in the un organized sector. It, therefore, deserves a serious scrutiny to assess its chances of success, and to highlight the modifications that may be required. To evaluate the features of the SSS it would be useful to compare it with any other existing scheme in the country. A similar scheme—the Integrated Social Security Scheme (ISSS)—has been operated on a limited scale by the Self-Employed Women's Association (SEWA), for over a decade. The evidence collected from the field in the course of operations of the ISSS would provide useful pointers for designing a viable government-sponsored SSS. Also, reviewing, SEWA's experience would help us evaluate the possibility of implementation of the SSS on a large scale through non-government entities.

SEWA's Integrated Social Security Scheme

SEWA launched the ISSS in 1992. This scheme covers the risks of death (natural or unnatural), loss of assets, maternity benefits and hospitalisation. The benefits include a coverage up to a certain monetary cap for some listed risks. This is a community-based initiative for participants from the informal sector, who are often from below the poverty line, and who almost always have irregular incomes. The ISSS covers 92,277 individuals out of which 23,214 have also opted for the health cover component, i e, 16 per cent of the membership of the ISSS opted for the health cover component. The ISSS has three variants with a premium of Rs 85, Rs 200 and Rs 400 respectively, linked to different packages of benefits. Within the composite scheme, a certain amount is earmarked for the health insurance component -Rs 37.50 in the case of the smallest benefit package under the ISSS (i e, 44 per cent of the total premium). Under the scheme services may be availed of from any type of service provider -private, public or private-not-for-profit. The reimbursement is in accordance with the norms and a fixed schedule of rates, irrespective of the actual expenditure incurred by the beneficiary. The average premium collected per individual for life insurance cover was Rs 50 and that for health insurance cover was Rs 118 in 2001-02. The average reimbursement under the scheme is approximately 50 per cent of the actual expenditure incurred. The insurance scheme was funded partly by the premium collected, partly through government subsidy and partly from the income obtained from a donated corpus. The premium collected from subscribers meets about 70 per cent of the expenditure on the integrated scheme. The premium: claim ratio for health insurance has ranged between 32 per cent and 83 per cent over the last decade, and was 38 per cent in year 2001-02. The operating cost of the integrated scheme (including promotion, marketing and capacity-building) was approximately 60 per cent of the total expenditure in year 2001-02. SEWA's experience shows that effort is required in close contact with the workers of the unorganized sector to convince them of the usefulness of a social insurance scheme, particularly one related to health insurance. It is difficult for illiterate or semi-literate workers to internalise the concept of paying for insurance cover for a contingency that may or may not arise in the future. SEWA's strategy has been to interface with the workers of the unorganized sector through local community leaders from the same sector. The process of educating the general community on the need for acquiring insurance cover is achieved through intensive advocacy and interaction between the community leaders and the workers.

It is clear from this that very high operating costs are inherent to social sector schemes that are targeted to make good the unmet needs of the most under-privileged. The ISSS, as a whole, taking into account the funds employed from all sources, has been found to be attractively viable. The average nominal return on investment (in the six years ending in 1999) was 12.3 per cent; and, even after factoring the impact of inflation in that period, the real rate of return on investment was 3.4 per cent. These figures are on the basis of calculations of financial rate of return. If one calculates the social rate of return, this would be much more attractive—the shadow value of benefits accruing to the unorganized sector would be much higher than mere monetary value. Looking at the health insurance component of the ISSS independently, the scheme is very viable, and in the case of SEWA assists by cross-subsidising the life insurance component of the ISSS to some extent. In a conceptual sense, the ISSS is a holistic social welfare scheme covering catastrophic financial contingencies arising from any major risk in the life cycle of the workers. In its totality, the ISS operated by SEWA is an extremely productive one. Looking to SEWA's experience, one would be inclined to indulge in the hope that the prognosis for the new state-sponsored SSS is favourable. The main features of the government-sponsored SSS and SEWA's ISSS have been described in some detail earlier. There are significant similarities between these schemes. When launched on a national scale, SSS would mark a major intervention in the social welfare sector. It would, therefore, be of interest to know what implications the scheme would have if it is implemented in its present form. To anticipate the likely outcomes, some broad observations on the principal features of SSS are offered in the subsequent paragraphs.

Under the SSS it is envisaged that the pension scheme component will be independently operated by the scheme administration, while the accident insurance cover and health care components will be off-loaded to other insurance agencies. The plan to off-load the responsibilities for major components does not bode well for the scheme. The private sector health insurance operations in the past have been extremely expensive and financially non-viable. GIC's Mediclaim scheme, with a average premium of Rs 717 per subscriber, has been a loss-making one. Also, private health insurance operations have only been carried out in urban areas where it is not difficult to enlist health service providers. A health insurance scheme with widespread coverage would require an implementation agency with an Organizational culture entirely different from a commercial Organization. Even otherwise, the ESIC is the Organization in the country with the richest experience in providing a health cover to a widely scattered subscriber group. In this backdrop, the SSS would enjoy the best prospects of success if it implemented the health insurance component through the EFPO/ESIC. The personal accident life cover risk may be off-loaded on to an insurance entity, but the subscribers should only be required to interface with the SSS administration. In other words, for the personal accident cover the SSS administration should act as the TPA. Subscribers from the unorganized sector would not ordinarily have the capacity to claim their benefits/ services from commercial Organizations which would have a natural tendency to resort to 'skimping' in order to maximise their profits. As a matter of principle, the legal relationship under the SSS should be between the scheme administration and the subscriber. The fact that the scheme administrator may choose to sub-contract some of the services to another agency, is only incidental. The scheme administration must always be in a position to intercede on behalf of the subscriber in the matter of accessing the benefits.

The scheme requires a very wide network of functionaries to implement it. The plan relies heavily on the existing EPFO network, local self government institutions and other non-governmental entities. The EPFO has had an indifferent past record even in the discharge of its existing duties. It is not possible to feel confident that this Organization will successfully take on a mandate that is several times more burdensome than the current one relating to the workers provident fund. Moreover, the nature of the activity would be completely different. The SSS is an insurance operation where risk and resources have to be pooled to maximise the value of the inputs. The work-culture of an Organization substantially engaged in a health security scheme has to be entirely different from that of an Organization in which funds are collected from different contributors and suitably invested to optimise return, while staying within an acceptable band of prudent investments. The principle activity under the SSS will be human resource-based. As is seen in SEWA's integrated scheme, over 60 per cent of the expenditure is the operational cost relating to advocacy, sensitisation of participants, cultivating of personal trust and capacity building of the community leaders who really serve as the insurance agents. In this background it is felt that it would be an over-optimistic expectation that the existing EPFO network, together with non-governmental agencies, would be able to run the scheme efficiently. The estimated operating cost of the scheme at 1 per cent has no grounding in reality. At this point of time the only Organization that has substantial experience in running a health security scheme, is the ESIC although this health scheme (which is for the formal sector) is poorly administered. In operating the health security; component of the SSS, the seed-experience of the ESIC can be used with profit. In fact, if the two cannot be merged for various administrative reasons, they can at least be made to work in tandem so that there is no overlap in their sphere of activities. In sum, the ESIC and the EFPO need not be two independent and parallel Organizations in the health security sector. For the health insurance part at least, the scheme administration would need to shoulder the bulk of the responsibility of directly contracting health service providers from the private and private- not-for-profit sectors, and of monitoring and regulating the quality of services. In course of time, when the other insurance companies/NGOs have designed schemes and have started working in line with the basic structure of the UHIS, certain blocks of subscribers can be off-loaded to them. However, the role of the scheme administration cannot only be of a coordinator between independent insurance agencies. To discharge this role, the SSS administration would certainly need earmarked staff, and would have to make administrative expenditure much beyond the 1 percent that has been assumed in the scheme. Therefore, the authorities should quickly return to the real world and formulate norms for staff both at the state level and at the decentralized implementation levels. If the staff is not available on a reasonable normative basis the scheme would be still born. Also, the staff earmarked or recruited for this work would need to be specifically trained with tailor-made modules to equip them for their work. Whether the scheme is tried out on a pilot basis or implemented on a wider scale, the work skills required would be entirely different from those in conventional government or commercial working.

In the case of the unorganized sector, employers are currently not required under any law to keep records. The new scheme envisages an elaborate set of responsibilities for the employers. If the employers were willing and cooperative in discharging such responsibilhies, there would be no difference between the organized and unorganized sectors. One reason for limiting the statutory coverage of the organized sector to establishments above a formative size was the practical impossibility of netting all employers under the existing law. The heavy responsibilities enjoined on employers under the new scheme seems to assume a much more effective level of enforcement of the new law over the so-called 'unorganized' sector. From a practical viewpoint, it is not easy to understand why such employers (in small and scattered establishments and family-centric activities) will admit to an employer-employee relationship and contribute their share to the scheme. The scheme proposes that an authorised officer under the new law will determine the status of the employee and the employer. However, the past record shows that unorganized workers have rarely been able to establish their rights vis-a-vis their employers, be it in the matter of tenancy or in claiming minimum wages. In the case of unskilled labour, where employment is shifting and for brief periods, this would be even more difficult. In this situation, for the first decade at least, it would be unrealistic to assume any significant contribution on the part of the employers. The proposed option in the SSS—that in cases where the employer cannot be identified, the worker may enroll in the scheme on payment of the employer's contribution in addition to his own—is scarcely a tangible relief. Even for the workers' own contribution, it would be unrealistic to expect them to be in a position to pay Rs. 600/1,200 (depending whether they are in group I or II) in one installment, on a given date. Some innovative concessions may have to be given by way of allowing multiple installments, or payment at harvest time, when even landless labourers enjoy better liquidity. Those workers, whose employers cannot be identified, would be amongst the poorest in the unorganized sector, and it would be difficult to expect a sizeable number of them to make the employer's contribution in addition to their own. In this background, the cost will have to be borne by the state, if this section is not to be entirely excluded. In fact, if in the pilot studies it is found that the poorest section is being screened out, the government should even consider increasing its subsidy to reduce the premium contribution on the part of the employee, so that this social sector initiative touches the lives of those who have least been benefited by national development so far.

The assumed component of premium for accident insurance is based on an actuarial calculation that is likely to be quite accurate. Mortality statistics relating to natural as also accidental deaths are to some extent robust. However, morbidity statistics in the country, particularly time trends, are virtually non-existent. This is one of the major handicaps faced by insurers in designing health insurance packages that are reasonably attractive to the beneficiary and are at the same time financially viable. The SSS has assumed a premium of Rs 548 per annum for a family of five, i.e., a premium of Rs 110 per beneficiary. Prima facie, this is grossly underestimated. Mediclaim has not broken-even with an average premium of Rs 717 while operating a scheme similar to the health insurance component of the SSS. Thus, the health insurance premium component would need to be considerably scaled up to give the scheme any chance of success.

The idea of having a composite scheme for old age pension, accident insurance and health, is conceptually a sound one.

Basically, the poor, particularly in the unorganized sector, require a safety net against catastrophic events that may occur in the course of their life cycle. Covering one of the risks, and not the other, would be of little use, as the occurrence of the uncovered catastrophe would still drag the individual into destitution. Therefore, for any social insurance scheme the attempt should be to cover as many of the catastrophic risks encountered in a life cycle as can be accommodated within the affordable premium.

Conclusion

The introduction of UHIS and SSS would be an opportunity for seriously pursuing workers' welfare schemes in the country. With the sweep of globalisation in the 1990s, the middle class has grown to a size of three hundred million; the aspirations of this section are also pitched on the global reference scale - they would not be looking for benefits under any workers welfare schemes. The economic elite, which is small, would also have no time for trying to access state-sponsored initiatives. This leaves close to seven hundred million population, a little less than half of which would be below the poverty line, and the balance, while being above the poverty line, would still be struggling economically. For this gigantic population slab, workers welfare schemes would certainly have some meaning. In the past, welfare schemes for the unorganized sector have been hurriedly strung together at short notice to give some shine to an otherwise colourless budget document. Both the birth and the demise of the schemes largely go unnoticed. A government that introduces a welfare scheme out of conviction, would have to drive it along relentlessly with a steady pressure. The UHIS and SSS, after a serious launch, would take, perhaps, two decades, before the benefits were equitably accessible to all who needed to access it. The contents of the package and the span of coverage can gradually increase over time. The question which is often raised about the UHIS is: if it requires such an elaborate arrangement over such a long period, why not rely upon the alternative of boosting the existing state-run health system. The answer is that the public health system would always be required and should never be contributing less than a minimum share, say, one-third of the aggregate health services required in the country. However, there is a widespread perception that beyond a certain size the public health system collapses under its own weight. With its existing mandate of meeting the comprehensive needs of the entire population, the public health system has acquired too much of Organizational rigidity and provides virtually no service in large parts of the country. In this situation, bringing in a mix of providers, including private and private-not-for-profit entities, is considered a more feasible arrangement. However, it needs to be reiterated that a significant share of the services would have to be retained with the public health system as a counterpoise to the possible market distortion by the private health system. International experience in the recent past—particularly in Chile and Uruguay—has shown that private insurance tends to throw up several forms of market distortion, such as: excessive usage of health services on account of 'moral hazard'; increase of inappropriate care; noticeable 'adverse selection' and 'skimming' in different situations, etc. The classic example of the risks of runaway private health system is that of the US. In that country, despite the fact that aggregate health expenditure is 14.5 per cent of a very high GDP, approximately fifty million individuals have no insurance cover and are perilously exposed to catastrophic illnesses. Therefore, in a developing country like India the public health services should continue to be a significant share of the aggregate health services, so that the country does not become captive to a distorted and inflationary private health system. At the same time, non-government agencies can be co-opted on a wide scale to implement social security schemes so that the burden on any one sector remains manageable.

4

Health Insurance for the Poor

Community based health insurance (CBHI) is more suited than alternative arrangements to provide health insurance to the low-income groups living in developing countries. The Universal Health Insurance Scheme, launched by the prime minister of India is only one of the forms that CBHI can take. While analysing the proposed scheme, we examine alternate forms of CBHI schemes prevalent in the country. The development of the private health insurance market in the country will not leave the poor unaffected. Insurance sector reform can affect the poor through its effect on the provision of health services (i.e., cost, quality and access) used by low-income groups as well as through its access to finance health care. In this paper we also explore how insurance sector reforms alter health insurance prospects for the poor in India, the changes on the health front that affect the poor or that are likely to take place as a result of insurance sector reforms. We conclude that in the diverse settings of India all forms of CBHI have a role to play and that they need to be encouraged by the government through appropriate interventions. Formal insurance providers can also be reigned in to serve low-income population. At the same time, developments in the formal health insurance market need to be guided so as to minimise cost escalation of health care provision.

Introduction

Health care financing in India can be considered almost unique in several respects. One, the share of public financing in total health care financing in the country is considerably low—just around 1 per cent of GDP compared to the average share of 2.8 per cent in low- and middle-income countries and relative to India's share in disease burden. Two, the beneficiaries of this limited public health financing are not only the poor as one would expect in the case of limited public spending, but also the well-oil section of society. Third, over 80 per cent of total health financing is private financing, much of which takes the form of out-of-pocket payments (i.e., user charges) and not pre-payment schemes. Reliance on out-of-pocket payments is not only inefficient and less accountable than other methods of financing, it is also iniquitous to the poor on whom the disease burden falls more disproportionately, and who are more susceptible to disease and likely to be pushed into the poverty trap [Cumber 1997, Visaria and Cumber 1994]. Peters et al (2002) estimate that one-quarter of all Indians fall into poverty as a direct result of medical expenses in the event of hospitalisation. One of the important challenges facing the Indian health policy experts is: how to convert predominantly private out-of-pocket spending into health insurance premium where this amount is collected from a much larger group of insured individuals rather than from the limited number households affected by illness. Another important challenge is: how to provide health insurance to the people who cannot afford to pay (full) premium. Before digging deep into the issues involved let us look at the broad health care financing options.

In financing of health services a country may, in principle, choose between public financing through general taxation or private financing through health insurance. Public financing is justified where equity concerns override the efficiency objective. Where the opposite is true, reliance is often placed on the private insurance market. Equity considerations in the private insurance market can generate inefficiency and market failure as they involve trade-offs between desired distribution and the distorted incentives that accompany such redistribution. Therefore, where equity is the prime consideration it can best be achieved under public financing. In practice no health financing system is either purely public or private. Countries where private health insurance dominates, some public financing can still be observed. Similarly, some private insurance can be seen even in a public funded health system. All insurance systems, public or private, must strike a balance between economic efficiency and equity.

The choice between public health financing as, private insurance is hardly available to countries like India because of the governments limited ability to marshal sufficient resources to finance health spending. This is also the case because the nature of employment (where majority of workers are self-employed, or do not have a formal employer or steady employment) is such that there is little scope for payroll taxes. Given this problem, heavy reliance on private spending is necessary for financial reasons, notwithstanding the declared policy of the state to provide universal comprehensive primary health services to the entire population. Private spending may also be desirable on efficiency grounds. But the form that the bulk of private spending takes need to change from out-of-pocket payments to private insurance.

Insurance or pooling of risks through pre-paid schemes has a number of advantages. Besides being more equitable, it is one of the significant drivers of improvement in health care provision by encouraging investment and innovation. Also, it helps to improve the quality and efficiency of the public health care system by continually benchmarking it. Private insurance has certain pitfalls too such as leaving out low-income individuals who may not be able to afford the premium, and denying coverage to people who are sick, and limiting the coverage for high-cost conditions or services. In a country like India where public health care suffers from poor management, low service quality, weak finances, and lack of responsiveness to patients' needs and demands, the development of health insurance is likely to bring about improvement in the public health care system. Even the private health sector in India has grown in an undirected fashion, with virtually no effective guidance on the location and scope of practice, and without effective standards for quality of care or public disclosure on practices and pricing [World Bank 2002]. Development of health insurance will necessitate improvement in the private sector as well. The pitfalls associated with private health insurance can be reduced through appropriate regulation. To the extent that a certain per cent of the population can be covered through private health insurance, it will tend to reduce the need for government financing of secondary and tertiary care. This will help the government to develop and maintain smaller and well targeted systems of health care financing to serve people who do not have access to private insurance, and to address public health priorities such as immunisations that are quasi-public goods [Srinivasan 2001].

Before launching any major health initiative, there ought to be a well articulated vision of health care system for the country, and public health policy must be devised to realise that vision. Ideally, certain basic health services, including inpatient care, must be made available to every member of society. These services must be paid through insurance, which means that every member must have a health insurance cover or at least have access to health insurance, with the government subsidising the insurance premium, in full or in part, for those who cannot afford it. For the upper- and middle-income population, private health insurance market with effective and sound regulation can take care of health financing. However, even with the development of the private insurance market only half the country's population can, at best, be reached. The other half, which consists of the low-income population (30 per cent of the population is below the poverty line and add to it another 20 per cent living dangerously close to this line) is likely to remain outside the ambit of private health insurance unless there is an explicit social obligation in this respect, which can come only from the insurance regulator. For the low-income population, who are the main focus of this paper, neither a government provided nor a market-mediated arrangement is appropriate. Community based health insurance because of its features such as the voluntary participation of people, not-for-profit objective scheme management by the community itself, and some degree of risk pooling, is more suited to insuring the poor (see Section II). The CBHI schemes themselves can take different forms. The forms that are prevalent in India are discussed further.

This paper is structured as follows: in the Section II. I discuss different forms of CBHI schemes prevalent in India, and critically examine the 'universal health insurance scheme' launched in the country recently. The development of private health insurance in the country will also have a bearing on the access to health care services by the poor. In section III I discuss the factors that are holding back the development of private health insurance in the country, and in Section IV I explore how the development of the private health insurance market could possibly affect the poor. Section V concludes the paper.

Health Insurance for the Poor

For the low-income populations, insurance was never considered as an option in the past. They were assumed to be too poor to save and pay a premium. Hence, the government assumed the responsibility of meeting the health care needs of the poor. One could argue that if the government pays for the poor anyway, why think of insurance at all? Instead, why does the government not continue providing free health services to the poor, as in the past? Well, the strategy of free public health provision has not worked well in most states. Shrinking budgetary support to the public health services, inefficiency in provision, and unacceptably low quality of these services is reflective of this problem. Even in states like Tamil Nadu where public health care provision is reasonably developed, and may even get better as the decentralisation process deepens, there are reasons for introducing health insurance. First, it is being increasingly realised that even low-income groups can make small periodic contributions, which can add up to a significant amount, thereby taking some pressure off from already strained state revenues. Second, the insured people would have the option of going to either a public or private service provider, which in turn would generate competition among providers for better services. Finally, health insurance can be used to promote certain desirable behaviour. For example, Aarogya Raksha scheme of Andhra Pradesh links family planning to health insurance.

Conceptually, a society can be thought of as consisting of two groups of individuals, those who can afford to buy health insurance that promises a certain 'minimum' level of benefit, and those who cannot afford to buy the 'minimum' benefit on their own and need some public subsidy. As mentioned above, the development of private health insurance may take care of those who can afford to buy insurance. For those who cannot afford it, alternate approaches with some public subsidy are suggested. However, while operationalising the idea, this conceptual distinction gets blurred. The government's attention gets confined only to those people who are below the poverty line (BPL). While those below the poverty line definitely need to be covered with government support, the non-BPL population with low-income also needs to be covered, with or without government support, since market insurance is likely to bypass this section a well. An important policy question here is: how best to target and reach this section of the population? One way is to redefine the BPL population so as to include low-income people as well. Another approach is to include the non-BPL population in the scheme meant for the BPL population, with a lower level of subsidy. Even though the government's approach is to support voluntary insurance rather than to expand the existing social insurance schemes, the following approaches may be suitable for different sections of the society. For the upper and middle income population social insurance and voluntary insurance are suggested as the two dominant forms of financing health care. The state's role is primarily to develop an appropriate legislative framework, to appoint an independent regulator, and to formulate procedures and regulations to avoid well documented market failures [Misra et al 2003]. Even for low-income groups who are employed in the formal sector, social insurance may be a hewer way of providing health protection. However, it is for the low-income population working in the unorganized sector and those people below the poverty line that alternate approaches are needed. One approach suggested in the literature, which is relatively straight forward, is to create a sickness fund for this section of society. The fund could be used to cover all hospitalisation expenses of such families in public facilities as well as designated private facilities. Misra et al (2003) estimate the size of the fund required to cover hospitalisation costs of a 300 million BPL population. Assuming that 4 per cent of BPL population requires hospitalisation every year and the cost per episode (at 1995-96 prices) is Rs 2,100, the size of the fund comes to Rs 25,000 million per annum. Misra et al (2003) revise this cost figure and arrive at Rs 40,000 million required to covering the hospitalisation cost per annum of the BPL population. If instead of directly bearing the cost, the government provides this group with health insurance the demand on government funds may come down significantly, as insurance helps to mobilise some resources mobilisation from the people themselves (for comparison of costs see community based universal insurance scheme' further in this section).

Health insurance for the poor can take different forms. It could be community based or non-community based like the 'Jan Arogya' policy of the government. Community Based Health Insurance can itself take several forms. Two types of CBHI schemes that are observed in India are: an NGO acting as an intermediary between a formal insurance provider and the insured community (for example, SEWA in Ahmedabad, ACCORD in the Nilgiris) and the NGO itself providing insurance to the target community. In the latter case, where an NGO itself insures the target population, the NGO may also be the health service provider (for example, Sewagram Hospital) or may have an arrangement with the health service provider (for example, Tribhu vandas Foundation). (For other differences between these CBHI schemes see Table 1). All these forms currently exist in the country but only in small pockets and need to be explored. Each of these forms may be relevant depending on the local conditions that vary considerably across regions. For as diverse a country as India, there can be no pan India model. Indeed, CBHI schemes could be designed in a number of ways, depending on the socio-economic characteristics of the target population, its health profile, and the health risks prevalent in the region. Even within states different schemes could be designed for different districts. This calls for a scientific approach which begins with good experimentation, and fine-tuning as experience accumulates. The decentralisation process initiated in the country with the 73rd and 74th constitutional amendment aimed at promoting local bodies panchayat raj institutions (PRIs), in rural areas and, 'nagar palikas' in urban areas has raised hopes of being able to reach the poor through community-based initiatives with some subsidy to those who cannot afford the costs [Gumber and Kulkarni 2001].

The real benefit of CBHI lies in keeping the transaction costs low, in designing a scheme suited to community needs, in influencing health behaviour through health education, and affecting the supply of health care. Popularising insurance among the low-income population requires conveying the idea, canvassing for it, collecting premium, verifying claims and then reimbursing these. In the case of formal providers, all these functions typically take up a significant part (at least 20 per cent) of premium amount. In CBHI schemes such costs can be kept low say to 5-6 per cent. This is because many of these tasks can be performed by the community members themselves. Besides, in poor communities the financial barrier is only one of the barriers in accessing health care. Often, there are many non-financial barriers that must also be overcome through the design of schemes, which ought to take into account the characteristics of the community. All these aspects can best be handled if the scheme is community based. Additionally, the problems of adverse selection and moral hazard that arise due to informational asymmetries too can be reduced by making use of local knowledge that is readily available among people living in close communities.

By its very nature, CBHI scheme can be designed to meet health care needs that are specific to a community. By this reckoning a Jan Arogya type of policy, which is not tailored to meet the needs of the target community cannot be very successful. There is no community participation in the scheme, and this type of policy is also more prone to abuse. Generally, a CBHI scheme is organized through an NGO that is conversant with the target community. A CBHI scheme where an NGO mediates between community members and the formal insurance provider seems to combine the participatory feature with the efficiency aspect that is characteristic of the formal insurance provider. However, some forms of CBHI also have important limitations. For example, where an NGO itself provides insurance (acts like an insurer) the ability of the NGO to have a pool of well diversified risk is limited. This in turn restricts the ability of NGOs to cover or insure a variety of risks facing the target population. Moreover, where CBHI schemes are critically dependent on external funding, extending the reach of these schemes then depends on the amount of such funding available. Furthermore, the insurance schemes launched either by national or state-level governments when elections are in sight tend to be populist or vote-catching ploys. Since such schemes have to be renewed every year, they tend to be dropped once the elections are over. It is to be seen whether the universal health insurance scheme belongs to this category.

Insurance Reforms and Health Insurance Prospects for the Poor

Where an NGO itself provides insurance to the target community, insurance sector reforms do not directly affect the formation of such schemes, though appropriate regulatory changes designed to encourage such groupings may positively affect their formation. The scope for introducing such changes is greater now than it was prior to liberalisation. Insurance reforms do affect non-community based schemes (where the government directs public insurance companies to offer a product to the poor with or without some subsidy from the government) as well as NGO mediated CBHI schemes (where an NGO ties-up with the formal insurance provider in ensuring certain benefit packages to the targeted poor, e.g., SEWA). Both these types of schemes were more likely when insurance was a public monopoly. Now with the introduction of competition, for-profit companies will voluntarily serve those segments and introduce those products that are profitable in descending order of magnitude to the company. Typically, providing insurance to the poor is not profitable and insurance companies are unlikely to take up this moral obligation on their own volition. Furthermore, even public insurers that have mostly entered into such commitments may no longer be willing to do so as competition in the market intensifies. The regulator imposed uniform obligation across all formal insurers can then improve the prospects of NGO-mediated CBHI or non-community based schemes for the low'-income population. The current social and rural sector obligation imposed by the Insurance Regulatory and Development Authority (IRDA) is on the insurance business in general and does not specifically apply to health insurance. Furthermore, this obligation does not require insurance companies to subsidise premium. This obligation is just to ensure that some amount of insurance activity also moves to rural areas and does not remain confined to big cities and towns.

In the past, the public insurer cross-subsidised policies meant for the disadvantaged sections of society. Now, for cross-subsidy to work properly, a uniform social obligation needs to be imposed on all insurance companies, and not only on public insurers. Such an obligation would then come from the regulator and not from the government. The regulator, for example, could mandate all insurance companies to offer a 'basic' benefit package covering maternal, preventive, catastrophic and chronic care at standard prices to the poor, especially in rural areas along with some subsidy from the government. In this case, the regulator may limit exclusions, mandate guaranteed renewal, and make accreditation of service providers public. Here too NGOs can play a crucial role as an intermediary between private insurers and the community. Whether having a uniform cross-subsidy obligation on all insurance companies is the most efficient way of reaching the poor is an open question. Generally, a subsidy that comes from the general revenue of the government is the most progressive option.

Moreover, if pre-payment schemes run by charity hospitals are also brought under the insurance regulator's supervision, they can give a boost to such managed care arrangements. If the legal constraint becomes a real obstacle for the expansion of managed care-oriented health insurance, the indemnity model may de facto get encouragement resulting in cost escalation and reduction in the potential market for private insurance [Ferreiro 2000].

Community Based Universal Health Insurance Scheme

Prior to the recent announcement of the proposed community based universal health insurance scheme by the finance minister of India, various state governments were contemplating launching health insurance scheme for the poor population. State governments intensified their efforts when a similar announcement by the central government a year ago (in the budget of 2002-03), did not take off. Without a sufficient knowledge base, state governments were trying to enter into an arrangements with the providers of medical services, public insurance companies and the target community, whereby insurance companies would reimburse treatment costs of the target community and governments would subsidise the premium for the insurance sold to the target community. Some state governments had thought of paying the premium through their general revenues while others had planned to cross-subsidise it by bringing state government employees under a Mediclaim policy (Punjab and West Bengal governments alone were thinking on these lines). With the announcement (in the budget of 2003-04) made by the then finance minister to launch community based universal health insurance scheme for the low-income population, state governments have put off their plans.

Before analysing the scheme that was launched, let us first look at some of its important features. The scheme comes in three different types: *(i)* Re 1 per day per year for an individual *(ii)* Rs 1.5 per day per year for a family of up to five members and *(iii)* Rs 2 per day per year for a family of up to seven members. Given this, the bias towards family enrolment, as opposed to individual, enrolment is obvious. What are the benefits provided? Well, in case of hospitalisation the scheme provides medical expenses up to Rs 30,000 per family, if an earning member falls sick the scheme also provides for the loss of livelihood at the rate of

Rs. 50 per day up to a maximum of 15 days, and in case of death of the earning head of the family due to personal accident, Rs. 25,000 is given to the nominee.

In all these options while the government provides a subsidy of Rs. 100 which, remains fixed whether it is an individual who buys insurance or a family of five or of seven. While the scheme is open to anybody who wants to participate in it, the subsidy is given only to BPL families. Moreover, the scheme is designed to cover not a poor individual/family on the Indian streets but persons who are members of groups such as cooperative societies, bidi workers, handloom weavers, etc. In other words, the proposed scheme is a group insurance scheme with a membership of at least 100 families. The scheme is not designed to cover the entire BPL population, at least not in the initial phase. If the scheme survives and does not get extended to include other BPL families, state governments will need to think of reaching those poor who are not a part of any occupation-based or self-help groups and for whom the scheme is currently intended.

Some other salient features of the scheme are: *(i)* individuals between the age of 3 months and 65 years can join the scheme, *(ii)* total hospital expense that can be reimbursed under the scheme for any one illness can be up to Rs 15,000, with a cap on the amount payable for different types of hospital expenses, *(iii)* a number of illnesses/situations are excluded, for example, maternity insurance is not included, and *(iv)* claims are to be settled either by an intermediary called third party administrators (TPAs) or by the insurance companies themselves.

In the way in which the scheme is designed, it cannot be termed as a community based scheme. The scheme is designed to keep transaction costs low. But here too, the presence to TPAs limits the scope of reduction in-transaction costs. Because the scheme lacks a 'community character' the other potential benefits of community based schemes cannot be reaped.

Table 1: Important Differences in CBHI Arrangements

Types of arrangement	*NGO is Intermediary*	*NGO is Manager*	*NGO is Provider*
Examples	SEWA/ACCORD	Tribhuvandas Foundation	Sewagram/VHS
Type of risks covered	Inpatient care & non-health risks	Inpatient care	Inpatient and outpatient care
Pre-existing/chronic conditions	Excluded	May not be excluded	Not excluded
Membership size	Medium to large	Small to medium	Medium to large
Availability of benefit	After certain period	At time of discharge	At time of utilization
Administrative costs	Moderate	Low	Low
Subsidy	External	External	Internal/external
Group formation	Occupation/ geography based	Occupation/ geography based	Geography based

Furthermore, a universal standard package of costs and benefits takes away the needed flexibility in designing a scheme appropriate to local conditions.

The scheme is expected to cover 10 million families that are below the poverty line in the first year. The government subsidy is capped at Rs. 1,000 million. Assuming all 10 million families get covered, the resource mobilisation that can be effected is in the range of Rs. 3,650 million to Rs. 7300 million, with considerable variation in the claims liability. An important point to note is that the scheme is designed on the assumption that even the poor can contribute some payment towards their health security and the amount that is sought to be mobilised is significant. If this scheme is to be made available for the entire BPL population of about 300 million, the extent of resource mobilisation that could be effected is quite significant indeed. Assume average family size to be five. There would be 60 million poor families (assuming 300 BPL population). If each family pays a premium of Rs 540 (i.e., Rs 1.5 x 365) per year, the total premium amount would be Rs. 32,400 million (540 x 60). Of this amount, the government's contribution by way of subsidy (of Rs. 100 per family) would be Rs 6000 million. So, the amount that could be mobilised from the BPL population would be around (Rs. 32,400 million-Rs. 6,000 million) Rs. 26,400 million. If we compare this figure with the amount estimated by Misra et al of Rs 40,000 million, around 65 per cent of the funds can be mobilised from the people themselves! However, there is a catch here. These estimates only pertain to hospitalisation costs whereas the costs involved in the case of health insurance are higher, as they also provide for wage loss.

In principle, both public and private insurance companies can participate in the above scheme. In reality, the participation of private insurance companies seems unlikely, especially when there are other more lucrative areas still to be tapped. Prior to liberalisation, when insurance was a public monopoly, the launch of such a scheme would have made perfect sense. Indeed, two health insurance products—Mediclaim and Jan Arogya —were launched at that time, and we are all too aware of the dismal record of these products. Now with competition at the market place, would encumbering public insurers not put them at a disadvantage? Even though the subsidy is being paid by the government to cover for any possible shortfall, the scheme is unlikely to attract even public insurance companies. One, claims liability under the scheme is open-ended whereas the government subsidy is capped. Two, public insurers showed total disinterest, even scorn, when a similar scheme 'Janraksha' was announced in the budget of 2002-03. Little surprise why the scheme failed to act off the ground.

Health insurance schemes for the poor should take care of not just inpatient or hospital care, as designed in the proposed scheme, but also of outpatient care. It is often suggested that insurance be provided only for inpatient care and that outpatient care be left outside the ambit of insurance. The reasons given are: people can, by and large, afford outpatient care because it is relatively inexpensive; it is the inpatient care that pushes people into the poverty trap; administratively it is difficult to include outpatient care; and, that outpatient care would lead to cost escalation. Ideally, both inpatient care and outpatient care should be covered, and the decision of whether or not a patient needs hospitalisation should be made professionally and not be a function of whether or not the patient has a health insurance cover.

For this reason the UNDP-sponsored experiments on community-based health insurance, launched recently, have also addressed the issue of outpatient care as well. The community character of CBHI schemes is used to tackle the problem of outpatient care as well [for other issues in the design of CBHI schemes see Ranson and Jowett 2003]. However, with the launch of the universal health insurance scheme, it is not clear how the prospects of an NGO negotiating a health insurance package for and on behalf of a target community, with the public insurance companies, would be affected.

In the current debate on health security, health insurance is made out to be a panacea for all the ills facing the poor. Health insurance, no doubt, has emerged as an important financing tool as it promises to mobilise some resources from the people themselves i.e. those who buy insurance. But health insurance, which strengthens the demand side, makes sense only when the supply of health care is reasonably well developed. Where this is not so, health insurance is meaningless. The supply of health care in the rural and remote areas of country far from satisfactory. Although public health care centres are pervasive, they have degraded over time in most states due to lack of funds, accountability and so forth. Any attempt at introducing health insurance for the poor must also be accompanied by the revival of health care facilities at these centres. The need for stepping up public health spending is endorsed by many expert studies. Unfortunately, the launch of the scheme is not accompanied by either an increase in public health expenditure or a commitment to reorient the. public health system, and this seems to suggest a lack of seriousness in providing health security to the poor [Sankar and Kathuria 2003]. Finally, both the provision and access to health care services should be part of a bigger health strategy which includes other public health programmes such as safe drinking water, sanitation, family planning, etc, as each of these are important determinants of health outcomes. In other words a comprehensive approach is needed. With a view to understand how the development of private health insurance in the country is likely to impact the poor, we now turn to the factors that are currently affecting its development.

Private Health Insurance in India

Unlike most OECD countries where private/social health insurance is the main source of health care financing, in India, and more generally in developing countries, most private insurance is a supplementary service. Health insurance, whether social or private, whether formal or informal, is extremely limited in India. Existing health insurance schemes in India are mandatory schemes, private (voluntary) schemes, employer based insurance, and schemes in the NGO/voluntary sector. All these schemes put together cover about 110 million people or about 11 per cent of the population [Garg 2000]. This number falls far short of the private health insurance potential that is estimated anywhere between 400 and 500 million people. What is holding back the realisation of this potential?

Although a number of private insurance companies have entered after the liberalisation of the insurance market in 2000, no significant change in health insurance has been observed either in terms of new health insurance products or in terms of the volume of business. The two health insurance products, namely, Mediclaim for the general public and Jan Arogya for the poor, launched prior to the liberalisation, have not shown any significant growth either in terms of volume of business or in the number of policies sold post-liberalisation (see Tables 2 and 3). The new general insurers have introduced slight variations of the existing Mediclaim and the new life insurers have introduced some health riders to their life policies. However, their-volume of business is negligible [GoI 2002]. Why has the scope of existing health insurance schemes in India remained limited? Two important reasons cited are:— *(i)* poor product design, and *(ii)* lack of vigorous marketing of the products in order to sensitise the public to the need for health insurance. The existing health insurance schemes are indemnity based products wherein the payment to the health provider is first made by the sick individual and this amount is later reimbursed (partly or fully) by the insurance company to the insured individual. A large section of the population that cannot afford such large payments at the time of illness, even if the payments are reimbursed later, does not feel attracted to this type of insurance. Furthermore, the scheme provides for reimbursement only in case of hospitalisation, and not for outpatient care, and for allopathic treatment and not for treatment under alternate systems of medicine. Reimbursement of hospital expenses exposes the policyholders to the 'service' of insurers which is far from satisfactory. Coming to the second reason, when the public is not always aware of the need for health insurance, vigorous marketing of schemes becomes essential for popularising the scheme. Finally, health insurance is not demanded for its own sake but for reducing the financial barrier to health services. In rural and remote areas where the supply of health services particularly inpatient facilities is weak the demand for insurance naturally becomes constrained.

More generally, why has the health insurance business remained underdeveloped in India? Why has no reputed global health insurance company entered the market? Impediments to the establishment and development of private health insurance stem directly or indirectly from government policies regarding insurance and the health care sector [GoI 2002]. The most important impediments arise from the supply side, i.e., from the health care providers. Lack of standards for diseases and treatment procedures (where these standards and procedures exist, their adoption is lacking); absence of rating and credentialling of providers; non-existence of a centralised database, lack of standardised billing, claims and proposal forms are some of the problems facing the health care industry.

Table 2: Mediclaim Policy

	1997-98	*1998-99*	*1999-00*	*2000-01*	*2001-02*
No of persons Insured	2783862.0	3534417.0	4894129.0	5623864.0	7784491.0
Premium (Rs in lakhs)	21569.6	27173.5	38040.7	51898.2	74204.5
Claims (Rs in lakhs)	18612.4	21810.3	33226.1	47152.8	62038.6
Claims/ratio (%)	86.3	80.3	87.3	90.9	83.6

Table 3: Jan Arogya Bima Policy

	1997-98	*1998-99*	*1999-00*	*2000-01*	*2001-02*
No of persons insured	2783862.0	3534417.0	4894129.0	5623864.0	7784491.0
Premium (Rs in Lakhs)	115.3	2880.0	6569.0	6800.3	9079.3
Claims (Rs in Lakhs)	97.1	2882.4	7978.0	6689.0	8818.2
Claims ratio (%)	84.3	100.1	121.4	98.4	97.1

On the insurance regulation side too there are some issues affecting the development of the market. For example, the minimum capital norm for exclusive health insurers is deemed to be lower than what is currently prescribed. Similarly, solvency margins and reinsurance requirements appropriate to health insurance—which is less volatile than property and casualty insurance—are deemed to be different from those applicable to other lines of general insurance business. Currently, the requirements that apply to the general insurance business apply to health insurance as well. Similarly, there are no minimum capital requirements and solvency norms for health care providers interested in establishing and running managed care schemes. Besides, the current Mediclaim policy distorts the balance between price adequacy and coverage and restricts the ability of competitors to come up with more balanced products.

Once the entry barriers are removed, additional regulations need to be put in place for the smooth functioning of the health insurance business. Even though insurance regulations are meant to ensure fairness, efficiency, and financial accountability in health insurance and are similar to those applicable to general insurance business, the health insurance business always involves additional regulations. These relate to meeting the social objectives of access, adequate benefits, and consumer responsiveness. Typically insurers tend to develop a number of underwriting and pricing practices to avoid accepting high risk customers. This kind of market segmentation is economically efficient but may be considered socially unacceptable. Often regulators ensure that equal access is available to the payers of health care and that companies do not exclude high-risk individuals or costly preexisting conditions. Moreover, health insurance contracts are typically more complex than other insurance contracts. Regulators need to ensure that consumers understand the provisions of the contracts and that contracts are written in a manner that is understood by the buyers.

Since health insurance is closely linked to health care provision, interventions required to correct these problems call for a coordination with other arms of the government such as the ministry of health and family welfare, and bodies like the Medical Council of India, and the regulators. Finally, the government's role in promoting or impeding private health-related investment is a key element in the growth of private health financing and delivery. Unless these issues are dealt with one cannot expect any significant development to take place in the health insurance business in the country.

Impact on the Poor

Developments on the health insurance front will not leave the poor unaffected. Even though private for-profit insurance companies are not expected to voluntarily provide a health insurance cover to the poor, the poor may still be affected on account of the influence of the development of health insurance on the supply of such services. Furthermore, the poor may also directly benefit if insurance regulations are specifically designed to achieve redistribution and equity objectives. At the minimum, the government must ensure that: *(i)* the liberalisation of the insurance market provides value for money for the direct beneficiaries *(ii)* the poor are not adversely affected the liberalisation [Peters et al 2000]. However, the government can definitely aim higher by ensuring that the poor too benefit from the developments in health insurance.

The likely impact of developing voluntary insurance for the poor is far from clear. There are both potential benefits and risks associated with it. The development of health insurance would influence the supply of health services both in terms of its quality and price. It would also influence the extent of public funds available for subsidising the poor. The potential benefits and risks are formally listed below:

Potential benefits: (i) If the introduction of evidence-based medicine trickles down to other providers that are used more often by the poor, the poor could benefit from the improvement in quality in the private sector; *(ii)* If public subsidy to the non-poor who join health insurance decreases, greater public resources may be available for providing subsidies to the poor.

Potential risks: (i) The gap between the access of the poor at present and the required access may increase with cost escalation. *(ii)* As the non-poor make a switchover from public to private hospitals there is a risk of political support for public financing becoming reduced which would impact the poor by excluding them that quality care in the private market or by deteriorating the quality of public services [Peters et al 2002].

The poor might benefit from the expansion of private providers if the supply of health care expands due to the rise in affordability resulting from health insurance. However, if prices grow faster than delivery capacity, cost escalation may expand even the existing gap between the poor and the required access to health care. All this is unpredictable, since it depends on the supply response of health care and the model of health insurance implemented in the country. Regarding the latter, it is clear that an indemnity/fee-for-service system will unavoidably result in a severe cost escalation whereas a managed care one, which coordinates financing and delivery of health care would probably be capable of keeping costs under control. Managed care by containing unnecessary treatment, helps in controlling of costs and thereby makes health insurance more affordable to a larger number of people. It also provides incentives for improving health care delivery, promotes preventive care such as medical checkups, immunisation and so on. Since the fee-for-service approach to payment of health providers tends to escalate costs the government should encourage managed care models.

The pro-poor recommendations made in the World Bank organized national seminar on the topic are: *(i)* reduce the public subsidy to the wealthy by charging full cost recovery to the insured who use private insurance, *(ii)* define a minimum package of services cover that include preventive, maternity, and catastrophic cases, *(iii)* encourage informal community financing schemes, for example, managed care schemes through NGOs with less regulation and lower capital deposit requirements.

Conclusions

Health insurance is emerging as an important financing tool in meeting the health care needs of the poor. Neither market mediated nor government provided insurance is an appropriate way of reaching the poor. Community based health insurance is a more suitable arrangement for providing insurance to the poor. The development of private health insurance in the country has both potential risks and benefits in the access of the poor to health services. Appropriate regulatory changes can minimise the risks and turn potential benefits into concrete gains for the poor. However, currently even the private health insurance market lacks development for the want of proper regulatory decisions both on the supply of health services and on the demand for health insurance.

CBHI, which is the more appropriate insurance arrangement for the poor, could take different forms and each of these forms may be suitable depending on the characteristics of the target population, their health profile, and health risks to which the community is exposed. Indeed, for a country as diverse as India there can be no pan India model and all different forms need to be explored. The scheme announced in the last budget and recently launched by the prime minister, seems promising provided the insurers find it attractive enough to partake in. The liberalisation of the insurance market has made this less likely, as competition in the market place will turn the focus of companies to the most profitable lines of business. However, a regulatory requirement to this effect may then be a possible way out. The proposed scheme being a group insurance scheme is not meant to cover the entire BPL population and it also excludes outpatient care. As experience accumulates, the scheme can be fine-tuned and expanded to cover the entire low-income population. However, increased public health spending and reforming of public health facilities is a must for the success of these community-based health initiatives.

Community Health Insurance in India—An Overview

According to the World Health Organization, greater than 80 per cent of total expenditure on health in India is private (figure for 1999-2001 [World Health Organization 2004]) and most of this flows directly from households to the private-for-profit health care sector. Most studies of health care spending have found that out-of-pocket spending in India is actually progressive, or equity neutral; as a proportion of nonfood expenditure, richer Indians spend marginally more than poorer Indians on health care. However, because the poor lack the resources to pay for health care, they are far more likely to avoid going for care, or to become indebted or impoverished trying to pay for it. On average, the poorest quintile of Indians is 2.6 times more likely than the richest to forgo medical treatment when ill [Peters, Yazbeck et al 2002]. Aside from cases where people believed that their illness was not serious, the main reason for not seeking care was cost. The richest quintile of the population is six times more likely than the poorest quintile to have been hospitalized in either the public or private sector [Mahal, Singh et al 2000]. Peters et al (2002) estimated that at least 24 per cent of all Indians hospitalized fall below the poverty line because they are hospitalized, and that out-of-pocket spending on hospital care might have raised by 2 per cent the proportion of the population in poverty [Peters, Yazbeck et al 2001]. Given this context, health insurance appears to be an equitable alternative to out of pocket payments.

In recent years, community health insurance (CHI) has emerged as a possible means of: *(1)* improving access to health care among the poor; and *(2)* protecting the poor from indebtedness and impoverishment resulting from medical expenditures. The World Health Report 2000, for example, noted that prepayment schemes represent the most effective way to protect people from the costs of health care, and called for investigation into mechanisms to bring the poor into such schemes (World Health Organization 2000). Various other terms are used in reference to community health insurance, including: 'micro health insurance' [Dror et al 1999], 'local health insurance' [Criel 2000] and 'mutuelles' [Atim C 2001]. We define CHI (along the same lines as [Atim 1998]) as any not-for-profit insurance scheme that is aimed primarily at the informal sector and formed on the basis of a collective pooling of health risks, and in which the members participate in its management." CHI schemes involve prepayment and the pooling of resources to cover the costs of health-related events.

They are generally targeted at low-income populations, and the nature of the 'communities' around which they have evolved is quite diverse: from people living in the same town or district, to members of a work cooperative or micro-finance groups. Often, the schemes are initiated by a hospital, and targeted at residents of the surrounding area. As opposed to social health insurance, membership is almost always voluntary rather than mandatory.

Internationally, there is a shortage of empirical evidence to assess whether or not CHI schemes have improved access and financial protection among the poor. Enthusiasm for such schemes was fuelled in part by studies showing disproportionate increases in utilization among the poorest with the implementation of insurance [Yip arid Herman 2001] or mandatory prepayment schemes [Diop, Yazbeck et al 1995] in developing countries. But studies of voluntary CHI schemes have yielded less promising results. The studies and reviews that have been undertaken suggest that many schemes are short-lived and fail even to meet the goals they set for themselves [Bennett, Creese et al 1998]. Often, the schemes enroll relatively small populations (of 1,000 people or less) thus limiting the extent to which there can be pooling and resource transfers (International Labour Office (Universitas Programme) 2002). Furthermore, CBHIs have tended to exclude the poorest among their target populations, in part because they generally charge a flat (or uniform) premium that is unaffordable to the poorest. Under the three schemes reviewed by Preker et al [Preker, Carrin et al 2001] in Rawanda, Senegal and India, even among the insured, low income remained a significant constraint to health care utilization.

The purpose of this paper is to describe Indian CHI schemes, jand where data are available, their impact—

it is intended to serve as an update on earlier work by one of the authors [Ranson 2003]. In India, community health insurance has a long history. The earliest such scheme was started in Kolkata in 1952 as part of a student's movement. The Student's Health Home (SHH) caters to the students in the schools and universities of West Bengal. Currently there are more than 20 documented CHI programmes, of which five were initiated in the past three years. Based on visits to twelve of the schemes, the authors describe the context in which they are operational, their design and management, the administrative challenges faced by them, and their impact. The names and locations of the programmes included in this summary are given in the accompanying table.

Underlying Objectives

Most of the insurance programmes have been started as a reaction to the high health care costs and the failure of the government machinery to provide good quality care. The objectives range from "providing low cost health care" to "protecting the households from high hospitalisation costs." BAIF, DHAN, Navsarjan Trust and RAHA explicitly state that the health insurance scheme was developed to prevent the individual member from bearing the financial burden of hospitalisation. Health insurance was also seen by some Organizations as a method of encouraging participation by the community in their own health care. And finally, especially the more activist organizations (ACCORD, RAHA) used community health insurance as a measure to increase solidarity among its members—"one for all and all for one."

Context

Almost all the 12 CHIs are based in rural or semi urban areas, working among the poor. This ranges from tribal populations (ACCORD, Karuna Trust, RAHA), dalits (Navsarjan Trust), farmers (MGIMS, Yeshasvini, Buldhana, VHS), women from self help groups (BAIF, DHAN) and poor self-employed women (SEWA). The size of the target population (i.e., the population from which they aim to draw members) ranges from a few thousands to 25 lakh (Yeshasvini trust). Most of them (eight of the twelve) use existing community based Organizations to piggyback the health insurance programme. While in some it is the existing self help groups (SHGs), e.g., DHAN, BAIF; in others it is a union (SEWA, ACCORD and Navsarjan). In two others it is the cooperative movement (Yeshasvini and Buldhana). These community-based Organizations have been a useful platform to explain the principles of health insurance to the community, for collecting premium and for managing claims and reimbursements. And most important, they have instilled a sense of ownership of the insurance programme among the community.

Table 1: CHI Schemes in India

Name and Location of the CHI As Well As Year of Initiation	*Target Population*	*Type*	*Remarks*
ACCORD Gudalur, Nilgiris, Tamil Nadu 1992	Scheduled tribes of Gudalur taluk who are members of the Adivasi Munnetra Sangam (AMS) - the tribal union. (N = 13,070 individuals)	I	Linked with the New India Assurance Company
BAIF Uruli Kanchan, Pune, Maharashtra 2001	Poor women members of the community banking scheme and living in the 22 villages around Uruli Kanchan town. (N= 1,500 women)	III	Linked with United India Insurance Company
BULDHANA Urban Cooperative and Credit society. Buldhana, Maharashtra	Farmers living in Buldhana District (N = 175,000)	III	Linked with United India Insurance Co.
DHAN Foundation Kadamalai block, Thane district, Tamil Nadu 2000	Poor women members of the community banking scheme and living in the villages of Mayiladumparia block. Total of 4,514 members and their families. (N = 19,049 individuals).	II	No linkages. The women operate the scheme by themselves.
Karuna Trust T Narsipur Block, Mysore District, Karnataka 2002	Total population of T Narsipur block and Bailhongal block, with a focus on scheduled tribes and scheduled caste populations. (N=634,581 individuals)	III	Linkage with National Insurance company
MGIMS Hospital Wardha, Maharashtra 1981	The small farmers & landless labourers living in the 40 villages around Kasturba Hospital. (N = 30,000 individuals)	I	No linkages. The Organization operates the scheme.

Navsarjan Trust Pathan District, Gujarat 1999 (discontinued in 2000)	Select scheduled caste individuals. In two blocks of Patan district, north Gujarat (N=?)	III	Linkage with New India Assurance Company
RAHA Raigarh, Ambikapur, Jashpur and Korba districts of Chhattisgarh 1980	Poor people living in the catchment area of the 92 rural health centres and hostel students. (N = 92,000 individuals).	I	Have their own providers
SEWA 11 districts of Gujarat 1992	534,674 SEWA Union women members (urban and rural), plus their husbands living in 11 districts. (N = 1,067,348 individuals).	III	Linkage with National Insurance Company
Student's Health Home Kolkata, West Bengal 1952	Full-time student in West Bengal state, from Class 5 to university level. (N=5.6 million students)	I	Have their own health facilities
Voluntary Health Services centre.	Total population of the catchment area of 14 mini-health	I	Have their own hospital and health
Chennai, Tamil Nadu 1972	Centres in the suburbs of Chennai. (N= 104,247 individuals in 2 blocks)		
Yeshasvini Trust Bangalore, Karnataka 2003	Members of the cooperative societies in Karnataka. (N = 25 lakhs)	II	Operate their own programme

In India, there appears to be three basic designs, depending on who is the insurer (see the Figure). In Type I (or HMO design), the hospital plays the dual role of providing health care and running the insurance programme. There are five programmes under this type. In Type II (or Insurer design), the voluntary Organization is the insurer, while purchasing care from independent providers. There are two programmes under this type. And finally in Type III (or Intermediate design), the voluntary Organization plays the role of an agent, purchasing care from providers and insurance from insurance companies. This seems to be a popular design, especially among the recent CHIs, with five of the 12 adopting this. The insurance companies are mostly the GIC subsidiaries, e.g., National Insurance Company, the New India Assurance Company, the United India Insurance Company, etc. Of late private insurance companies like the Royal Sundaram, and ICICI Lombard have been involved with CHI programmes.

As most of these programmes serve the rural poor, the premiums also have been low; in the range of Rs 20 to Rs 60 per person per year. Only three programmes had premiums higher than Rs 100 per person. The premium is usually paid as a cash contribution once a year during a definite collection period. Two schemes (RAHA and MGIMS) allowed the community to pay equivalents in kind. The community and their representatives as well as the staff of the voluntary Organization helped with the collection of the premium, e g, at Yeshasvini, the premium collection is organized through the existing cooperative infrastructure. Enrolment to the insurance programme ranged from a thousand to seventeen lakhs (Yeshasvini).

At most of the schemes, the unit of enrolment is the individual and membership is voluntary. While some of the schemes encourage family membership by providing a family package/rate (e.g., DHAN, Vimo SEWA and VHS), none requires enrolment of the whole household. However, several of the schemes do enroll groups rather than individuals—enrolment in these same schemes is to some extent 'mandatory', and they come to resemble social insurance schemes as a result. At Karuna Trust, for example, the cost of the premium is entirely subsidised for the poorest among the target population—the BPL-SC/ST—who are automatically enrolled in the scheme. Some of the self-help groups at DHAN purchase insurance for all SHG members (generally 15 to 20) out of profits earned by the SHG (i.e., certain SHGs have chosen to make the scheme mandatory). At SHH, once a school or institution registers, then it becomes mandatory for all the students to pay the premium.

As stated earlier, while some of the CHI schemes limited the benefit package to only ambulatory care, the twelve studied by the authors all provided inpatient care. Some also provided out patient care as well as outreach services. It is observed that the community prefers to have both outpatient and inpatient care. Most schemes had important exclusions like pre-existing illnesses, self-inflicted injuries, chronic ailments, TB, HIV, etc. One scheme covered only surgeries, all other medical conditions being excluded. While most of the schemes reimbursed direct costs of treatment (consultation, medicines and diagnostics), one scheme (Karuna Trust) also reimbursed loss of wages for the patient. Some CHIs had also added other benefits, e g, life insurance, insurance against personal accident and/

or asset insurance into the package to make it more attractive to the community.

In the Type I CHIs, there is a cashless system of reimbursement. However, in the other two types, usually it is a fixed indemnity with patients having to settle bills and then getting it reimbursed 2-6 months later from the NGO. The exception was the Yeshasvini scheme, which, though a Type III scheme, had managed to negotiate a cashless system with the private sector by using the services of a Third Party Administrator (TPA). Most of the CHIs have a fixed upper limit, ranging from Rs. 1,250 to Rs. 1,00,000 per patient per year.

Most of the providers are from the private sector - either for profit or not-for-profit hospitals. Only one CHI (the Karuna Trust) had a public sector provider. In the Type I schemes, where the insurer is also the provider, there is an attempt to maintain quality and keep costs down. For example at ACCORD, the hospital largely uses only essential and generic drugs. However, in the Type II and Type III schemes, where the provider is mostly the private sector, we did not find any evidence of cost containment or quality checks. Yeshasvini was the exception, where they have managed to negotiate capitation fees for each surgery. At SEWA, there is an ongoing initiative to empanel select hospitals (primarily government and trust hospitals) judged to be providing a high standard of care.

As stated earlier, most of the schemes are administered by the community, their representatives or by the voluntary Organization staff. This helps keep costs down. Usually they handle the following activities:

Creating awareness among the community; collecting

premium (at ACCORD, the sangam leaders collect the premium and hand it over to the NGO); monitoring for fraud (DHAN has an insurance committee comprising of SHG members who scrutinise every single claim); submitting claims; and channelling the reimbursements (at BAIF, the reimbursements are sent to the local SHG who while handing over the amount to the patient, reinforces the benefit of insurance). All these activities help in increasing the efficiency of the scheme. Also it helps build a sense of ownership among the community and increases accountability.

One of the weaknesses of the CHIs is the lack of techno-managerial expertise. This is reflected in the fact that most of them do not have inbuilt mechanisms to prevent adverse selection or moral hazard. Due to the asymmetry of information, it is possible that only the sick enrol in these schemes (adverse selection). Simple measures like a larger enrolment unit, a mandatory enrolment, a definite collection and waiting period are measures to prevent this. While all (except VHS) have a definite collection period, other measures are usually not used. SHH to a certain extent overcomes adverse selection by using the institution as an enrolment unit.

Similarly, because of the insurance programme, the behaviour of the patient or the provider may change (moral hazard). Capitation fee structures, standard treatment guidelines and copayments are some strategies to prevent this. The only measure consistently used by most -CHIs to reduce the patient induced moral hazard is co-payments and deductibles.

The absolute number of enrolees varies tremendously, from only 909 at BAIF (scheme is only in its second year) to as many as seventeen lakhs at the Yeshasvini programme. The average subscription rate varies from 10 to 50 per cent of the target population. Except at Vimo SEWA, there has been no study as to why the rest of the target population are not subscribing, but during the interviews, some of the reasons for not paying were elicited. These included:

(1) No immediate benefit; *(2)* premium too high; *(3)* "we are well, why should we pay in advance? When we fall sick, we shall pay"; *(4)* large families - this is specially since most of the CBHI's unit of membership is the individual; *(5)* "(Insurance scheme) Hospitals are far away and so we have to pay a lot to access hospitalisation. Better use the premium money to go to a nearby doctor"; and *(6)* "we pay every year, but do not get any benefit out of it. So we have decided not to pay any more". There is tremendous variation in terms of claims submitted annually for inpatient care, ranging from only 1.4/1,000 insured per annum to more than 240/1,000 insured per annum. Among schemes with the highest rates of utilization, adverse selection appears to be responsible for the high rates.

Among schemes with low rates of utilization, it appeared that not enough had been done to address non-financial barriers to accessing health care. The indirect costs of health care are not addressed by the schemes (Karuna Trust being an exception), and in many of the schemes, the direct costs are only covered up to a 'cap' or 'ceiling' (as at DHAN, RAHA and SEWA). Even at those schemes that do not have a cap (e.g., SHH), non-financial barriers may prevent people from utilising the scheme (e.g., distance, lack of knowledge about the scheme, limited awareness of health/illness, etc.)

In terms of their ability to protect individuals and households against the catastrophic costs of health care, the schemes again seem to vary considerably. Those that provide the greatest degree of protection have the following characteristics: (1) Cover 100 per cent of the direct costs; (2) cover all (or at least some) of the indirect costs; (3) cover all kinds of illness (e.g., all non-elective causes of hospitalisation, including complications of delivery, chronic illnesses); and (4) provide benefit right at the source of health care, i.e., with no period during which the patient has to cope with the costs of care. Thus, it was generally the Type I schemes, which provide health care directly, and usually with no upper limit to the financial benefits, that provided the greatest degree of protection. An important question is about the financial viability of these 'small' schemes. Of the 12 studied, four (BAIF, DHAN, Buldhanha and Yeshasvini) are run purely on funds raised from the community. All the Type I schemes have supplemented the locally raised resources with external resources (either from the government or donors). These external resources range from 20-40 per cent of the total reimbursements. Only two have relied exclusively on external resources. Unfortunately, it was difficult to get accurate financial estimate of the administrative costs, especially since a lot of this is subsidised by the community.

Financing health care has always been a very difficult exercise. "Even in rich countries like the US, there does not seem to be enough for all. It becomes all the more challenging in a low-income country like India. While the Constitution of India promises to provide adequate health care to the population, successive governments both at the state and the centre have failed in many ways to do so. This is probably one of the reasons why the majority of the public turns to the private sector for their health care needs.

Another equitable method of health financing is the social health insurance—seen in most European countries. Given the low percentage of workers in the formal sector, this appears to be a distant dream. However, these European (and Japanese) social health insurances have actually evolved from a conglomeration of small 'community health insurance schemes'. Historically, during the peak of the industrial revolution, worker's unions developed health insurance mechanisms to protect their members. This gradually developed into today's social health insurance [Ogawa et al 2003; Barnighausen, et al 2002]. Thus community health insurance can be seen as an important intermediate step in the evolution towards an equitable health financing mechanism.

The community health insurance programmes in India offer valuable lessons for the policy-makers and the practitioners of health care. While many state that the poor in India cannot understand the complexities of health insurance and will not accept any insurance product, we hereby document 12 schemes where health insurance has been operationalised. It is clear that what is required is a good product. Some of the conditions that have allowed these schemes to succeed are:

- An effective and credible community based Organization (or NGO). This is absolutely necessary as it is the foundation on which health insurance can be built. The CBO helps in disseminating information about health insurance and more importantly helps in implementing the programme with minimum costs.

- An affordable premium—this is very important. While most health insurance products (even for the poor) have premiums in the range of Rs. 100 plus per member per year, we find that people are willing to pay only in the range of Rs. 20 to 60 per person per year. This is significant, and needs to be taken into account by the insurers if they want their products to penetrate the rural market.
- A comprehensive benefit package is necessary to convince the community of the benefits of health insurance. Most of the CHIs documented, especially the Type I schemes have provided a comprehensive package and this is one of the main reasons why people have enrolled in their schemes. Unfortunately, most of the Type III schemes (except for Karuna Trust) have been forced to introduce exclusions by the insurance companies. While most insurance companies introduce exclusions, based on economic reasons, one has to look at health insurance within a public health context. Diseases like TB, HIV and mental illnesses have significant public health importance and should be covered. Similarly it is ironic that while the country has invested tremendously in safe deliveries, most health insurance products do not cover it. And finally as India enters an epidemiological transition and will have to encounter chronic diseases like diabetes and hypertension, it becomes imperative that these diseases are included in the benefit package.
- A credible insurer is imperative for people to have faith in the product. This is where the NGOs

and the CBOs score as they have a relationship with the community and so the people are willing to trust them with their money. Insurance companies need to learn from this important lesson and would need to approach the rural sector keeping this in mind.

- And last but not the least, the administration load of the scheme on the community should be minimal. Unnecessary documentation lead to frustration. In one of the schemes a community member mentioned that she had to pay more to get the certificates than she got in reimbursement. This is where the Type I and Type II schemes score over the others.

Many would dismiss community health insurance as a drop in an ocean. It may appear insignificant, given the scale of the problem in India. But, one needs to look at it in context. One of the main lessons from these case studies is the fact that a good community based Organization can help develop an effective community health insurance programme. And India is teeming with such Organizations—be it the trade movement, or the cooperative movement. So upscaling should not present a problem if one uses these existing institutions. Already there are examples of community health insurance being introduced in the dairy cooperative sector (Mallur, Karnataka and Anand, Gujarat); the head loaders union (Mathadi trust in Mumbai), shop owner's union (Palakkad, Kerala). The possibilities are endless, if approached properly.

However, one needs to mention a word of caution. The main pitfall in developing community health insurance is to find an appropriate provider. The Indian private health sector is unregulated and unaccountable

[Bhat 1999]. In this context, introducing health insurance can lead to uncontrolled cost escalation without the promise of quality [Ranson and John 2001]. So it becomes imperative that while considering community health insurance, one should seriously consider mechanisms to introduce measures for cost containment, assuring quality and ensuring standard treatment practices. And this is where the CBO (or NGO) can play a crucial role, by countering the power of the providers. The CBO could negotiate with the providers and develop a package that is conducive for the patients and the CHI."

Yet another issue is the legality of these schemes, given the new Insurance act (IRDA Act 1999). Currently the act does not acknowledge the presence of these schemes and their role in the larger insurance market. This could also be the reason why many of the newer schemes have linked up with the formal insurance companies—to legitimise their activity. But in the process, they may have lost on the flexibility and innovations necessary for a successful CHI.

The other issue that needs to be addressed is that of financial sustainability. The very fact that many of them have been operational for more than a decade, itself is proof that it may be a sustainable form of health financing. While accurate financial [data about the schemes were not available easily, rough estimates show that they are able to raise about 60 to 100 per cent of their resources. This has important policy implications, as it gives an indication towards the amount subsidy required to make these schemes viable. And given the fact that most of these schemes target the poor, it is important that the government comes forward to subsidise this equitable health financing mechanism.

In a country with one of the highest out of pocket health care expenditure in the world, it is imperative that some measures be instituted to protect the poor. We suggest that community health insurance could be an interim strategy to finance the health care of the people; till a more formal social health insurance is in place. We also suggest that this is a feasible alternative given that community based organizations and movements exist in India. What is required is to regulate the providers and to legislate so that the community health insurance programmes find a space within the Indian insurance context.

6

Jowar Rural Health Insurance Scheme in the Spirit of Sarvodaya

The idea for the scheme started from the Medico Friends Circle (an informal group that is concerned about issues of public health importance) students group that Ulhas Jajoo initiated in MGIMS, Sevagram when he joined as faculty there in the department of medicine soon after completing his masters from Medical College, Nagpur in 1976. The group would regularly meet and discuss the various issues of relevance in medicine. Fed up of their indoor discussions and ideological debates, the group decided to move out into the community and work with them. The students divided themselves into groups, which went to four different villages, one of which was to be chosen for proposed fieldwork. The students finally zeroed in on Nagpur village, which was around five kms away from Sevagram hospital because of practical considerations, and not the other village like Pujai which though needy but was quite far away and transport facilities to which were abysmal. It was the first lesson that roads and transport are related to health care.

The group initially talked to villagers about their health needs. In consultation, it was decided to run a dispensary in the local school on a weekly basis. They decided against using drug samples given by medical representatives because it was unethical. A small token amount was collected towards the drug bank from the villagers and the dispensary was started. The drug selection was based on effectivity, cost and toxicity; generic drugs were used. In the process, the group could get an insight of the exploitative drug market.

However, pretty soon the drugs ran out and on analysis, the group realised that the rich of the village were not paying up and it was actually the poor who had paid regularly. In the next village meeting, this was brought up and addressed. The rich felt hurt for being exposed publicly but then the flow of money became more regular.

Realising that some kind of regular follow-up was needed, it was decided to have a village health worker (VHW). Initially, they thought that the traditional 'dai' could be given this responsibility but they realised soon that the community did not give her enough credibility. It boiled down to selecting a male health worker, from the community who was not necessarily poor. Also, he needed to be respected by the community to be able to provide a leadership role.

It was also decided that only those who could pay would be allowed to access the services at the dispensary. This led to a situation where the absolutely poor were not able to access the services. To cater to this target population, which needed support, the scheme was linked to the hospital which would help in sustenance of the scheme. Sushila Nayyar, the director and founder member of MGIMS agreed to a policy that any person from the scheme would get free treatment from the hospital.

The next step was the establishment of a village fund. Jajoo had visited various health projects before initiating this scheme and these visits had shown him that the main reason for starting these projects was on compassionate grounds. The all-enveloping love often created dependency among beneficiaries. It breeds relationship of a 'doler' and the 'beggar'. Moreover, these projects were so heavily financed that their replicability was not possible [PRIA 1986]. Ulhas Jajoo did not want donations from outside to finance the health care (based on the feeling of 'charity corrupts people'). The purpose of the fund was not to raise financial support to the outreach programme, but to generate demand for qualitative service from the providers; in fact it was a tradition among villagers to collect voluntary contribution graded according to capacity for religious village function, sport competition or for temple construction. The fund would finance the salary of the VHW and the drug requirements of the local dispensary, besides transportation cost of the mobile health team. Since *Jowar* (sorghum) cultivation was quite common and it was easy to contribute in kind, it was decided to accept the contribution in the form of *jowar*—the contribution would be according to capacity and the services according to need (the poor needed more support).

The fund would act as a pre-payment scheme subscription, entitlements being free primary health care and subsidised referral care [Jajoo 1993]. A minimum amount was decided which would have to be paid by every family and also an additional amount of jowar would be charged depending on the kind of work the family members were engaged in or on additional holdings. At present the health insurance contribution from the lowest income group (landless labourers) is 12 *payali* of jowar per family per year (a *payali* is a measure equivalent to 1.25 kgs and a *payali* of jowar sells for around Rs. 4 at present market rates).

Since this ensured that uniform health care would be available to all those who paid for the village fund, some of the rich farmers felt that they were financing the health care of the poor and did not pay up. Thus, only 60 per cent of the village was paying up for first year. This was brought up at the next village meet. To ensure payment, it was made clear that only those who contribute will get the benefits of the scheme. The persons from the village who had paid would get free treatment, but who did not contribute to the village fund would have to pay for the treatment. Those who had not paid (after treatment) and absconded would he held accountable by the village and made to pay.

To prevent misutilization of services at the hospital, it was decided that 25 per cent of the costs of elective admissions like cataract, hernia, normal pregnancy would have to be paid by the patient, while the treatment for an emergency/unpredictable illness would be free at the hospital.

Gradually over the years, as scheme gained credibility, the coverage of the scheme grew from 60 per cent to 75 per cent and finally 90-95 per cent. The village fund would pay for the drugs in the local dispensary, the VHW's salary and the visit of the hospital vehicle once in three months.

The meetings in the village *(gram sabhas)* about various aspects of the scheme would be held every year before jowar collection and there would occasionally be 'stormy' and heated discussions. This gram sabha would serve a dual purpose of evaluating the performance of the health structure and also take disciplinary action on irregularities committed by the villagers themselves. The gram sabha helped to facilitate communication between the health system and the beneficiaries on one hand, while on the other it helped the villagers have their say with regard to the VHW and the health team; the gram sabha could also decide to change their VHW [Jajoo 1993]. The scheme helped the community have a right to demand good quality care from the system. It also ensured politeness and better behaviour in the hospital on the part of the providers.

On the basis of the lessions learnt from Nagpur, the team extended the health insurance scheme to other villages (presently there are 40 villages within a radius of 25 kms around the hospital, covered under the scheme).

Initially the VHW was paid a fixed amount in the form of jowar, but later on it was decided that the honorarium would be decided in the village depending on the VHW's work performance, whether he had been helpful and accompanied the patients in the time of the need. This was to bring some accountability to his/her work.

As the scheme slowly started spreading to other villages, each village opened an account with a 'withdrawal by cheques' facility. All the jowar collected as premium would be sold and the money would be deposited in this account as the village fund. At the end of the year, the money remaining in the accounts would be transferred to the village fund for the next year—occasionally, a part of the fund would be transferred to the Kasturba health society to form a common pool of money for all the villages—a corpus, the interest of which could be used for procuring drugs (centralised distribution from the hospital). The money would also be used for organising educative camps and 'Prabhodan Saptahs' (educative lecture week series) where non-health related topics including social/spiritual issues would be discussed.

Only 10 per cent of the expenditure on the scheme was recovered form the contribution in the form of premium and 90 per cent of the cost came from the hospital. Since the MGIMS hospital runs predominantly on government financing, which is public money, it was felt that this would be an appropriate utilization of the same. The structure of the scheme revolves around: *(i)* accessible hospital services of optimum quality; *(ii)* accountability of health care system to the consumers; and *(iii)* affordability of the services to the poorest [Jajoo, unpublished 'Towards an Appropriate Maternal Care'].

Jajoo and MGIMS realise that the sustainability of the scheme (that it has to cater to the poor) without external support is not possible. It was and is their belief that the government needs to support these kind of schemes and subsidise them as a part of its social responsibilities. Social financing has the following, spin off benefits: *(i)* it increases the accessibility of the health services; *(ii)* it promotes the operators concern of the health in the community; *(iii)* it generates the concept of the right to demand a quality health care by the beneficiary population; *(iv)* it responds to priorities as judged by the community; *(v)* it ensures that the services are acceptable; *(vi)* it keeps the service providers on their toes; *(vii)* it stimulates Organizational self-confidence and paves the way for participatory culture at the community level [Jajoo unpublished Towards an Appropriate Maternal Care'].

At this stage, the prerequisite for adopting the scheme was—at least 75 per cent of village families should contribute for the village to be insured. The scheme found acceptability among villagers and once they insured, did not look back in the years to come.

It was at this time when the scheme extended focus from curative care .to preventive and promotive health aspects. The strategy of cluster immunisation to achieve herd immunity was successfully implemented for vaccine preventable illnesses. The village sanitation was addressed by evolving an appropriate; model of latrine. 'One house—one latrine' scheme aimed at 100 per cent coverage of village families. It was not a dole. The part contribution in cash came from the villager beneficiaries and the rest from gram panchayat and state funds. The model found acceptance of the state and central governments for its replication.

Poverty being the greatest evil behind most health problems, as a logical corollary, the scheme extended its web to income generation programme, addressing village as a social unit for development. All familes in a village were offered membership of a cooperative society for dairy development or lift irrigation scheme for agriculture wherever feasible. The latter initiative could come through bank funds. The constitution of cooperative society was framed in such a way that decisions could only occur with no less than 75 per cent majority, thus making elections obsolete.

At this'stage village health insurance scheme underwent its first qualitative change. In addition to 75 per cent participation, at least one of the following criteria was needed for eligibility: *(i)* participation in 'one house—one latrine' scheme with near 100 per cent coverage of village families; *(ii)* organising lift irrigation scheme for all village families; *(iii)* organising milk cooperative for all village families; and *(iv)* electing village panchayat by consensus.

Organization of people through income generation schemes became a focus issue, benefiting the whole community. The eligibility criteria now heavily weighed in favour of community action. The health insurance scheme had now reached a stage where it was helping and initiating action-oriented culture in the village. The changed face of the insurance scheme gave impetus to 'one house—one latrine' scheme in many villages.

The various schemes available to the village are:

- Jowar insurance scheme—under this 50 per cent subsidy is given on outpatient care and 100 per cent on all indoor care except for elective admissions (50 per cent subsidy).
- Subsidised family insurance scheme for rural area (Rs 15/ person/year) when 75 per cent of village families contribute. In this scheme outpatient and impatient services are provided with. 50 per cent subsidy. The village need not fulfil the above enlisted criteria for enrolment.
- Indoor insurance scheme in which there is no insistence on 75 per cent of village families to contribute. The contributions are at the rate of Rs. 15/person/year. There is no outpatient

subsidy offered, inpatient charges are subsidised by 50 per cent.

- The hospital runs a health insurance scheme for families living in semi-urban pockets and in Wardha town, at the rate of Rs. 150 per year for a family of five. The entitlement includes 50 per cent subsidy in outpatient and inpatient charges.

Income generation programme became quite successful and brought in visible economic upliftment, but with it vices like alcohol, gambling, fierce party politics and competitiveness found inroads in the village. The police frequently raided and also visits to judicial court rose. It was a lesson to be learnt—cultural development must race ahead of economic upliftment for effective change. It was a turning point for the ethos of health insurance scheme.

If the ultimate aim of the health insurance scheme is organising people at the lowest ebb of society, we opted for women's self-help group (SHGs), since the women in poor families are the 'proletariat of the proletariat' (as quoted by Dada Dharmadhikari). The women are hardworking among all classes and the ultimate sufferers. They are also culturally sane. The Organization of this culturally sane section of society found its initiative in the early 1990s.

The organization of women into SHGs was need-based, so that their dependence on money could be addressed by forming collectives that would be able to provide economic support when needed. It was noticed that the women would stand by each other and there would be transparency, leading to more accountability. The culture of decision-making by consensus was thoughtfully inculcated in SHGs. As the money started coming (linkages with bank), women's status in family changed as she was now looked upon as a bread winner for the family too. The process helped empowerment of women.

By now it was realised that though health care offers an ideal medium to get entry in village life (albeit costly), organising the entire community around it had not taken roots, simply because it was not and is not the priority need of the masses. Illness as a calamity affects individuals and it is rare to find epidemics sweeping the community around which a sustained mass action can be initiated.

The income generation programmes attract people as they serve their individual interest. Since the programmes addressing all village families were chosen (lift irrigation and milk cooperatives), everyone came together to harvest the gains, creating a false impression of an organized community. In fact these programmes inculcated competitive lifestyle and the greed that comes with it. The realisation dawned, that short of cultural ethos, mere economic upliftment treads the wrong path.

The health insurance scheme had now reached a stage where it was helping to identify not only the action-oriented culture of the village but also action-oriented individuals with capacity to do good. All are not equal in a village; some are more revered than others. The culture evolution needs active participation of these revered ones ('sajjan samarth'). With aim to organise them, the focus of health insurance scheme shifted to individuals and families than the earlier insistence on an entire village. Action plans for individuals now emerged like—organic farming and 'vastra swavalamban' (cloth self-sufficiency). These are acts of faith. For an intelligent direction of this kind study circles (Prabodhan) became the need of the hour. It could not have been classroom learning but experiential sharing.

Educational talks based on experiential wisdom were organized after the month of February, when the crop harvest was over. The usual site was the temple, after 'arati' was over at 8 pm. A discussion would be initiated on issues relating to day to day lives, linking them to social-cultural values. Organic fanning was encouraged. The 'role models' in various fields were put before the community. Educational trips to the chosen role model's workplace helped people imbibe goodness. Thus evolved programmes aimed at *vastra swavalamban* and sustainable agriculture.

The focus of the scheme now shifted to organise and empower the revered ones. It aimed at breaking their culture of silence with a hope that reins of power be vested in moral leadership. It is from this empowerment and leadership that the anti-liquor movement has taken roots in the villages around Sevagram.

The jowar insurance scheme underwent a major conceptual change, focusing on individuals and families than the entire village. The family had to fulfil at least one criteria for eligibility of enrolment: *(i)* member of the SHG; *(ii)* experimenting organic farming; *(iii)* taken a vow for *vastra swavalamban*; and *(iv)* active member of study circle in the village.

When the scheme began in 1979, the focus was on curative care; later on it became preventable care; it then reached the stage of promotive care through income generation schemes; the focus moved on to being social and now it is to encourage moral issues in society.

Those that give priority to moral issues are insured under jowar scheme, while the rest can choose any of the other schemes listed above.

The changing focus gave impetus to SHG movement. SHGs were linked to banks, enabling them to offer crop-loans to the members. Being an unregistered body, it entirely runs on faith. It selects office-bearers by consensus who by rule, do not stay in office for more than two years. All codes of conduct were evolved through group discussions. The culture of decision-making by consensus and transparency in all transactions buttressed the faith women enjoyed among themselves. Since it enjoyed credibility of a dependable source of financial support, hence it did not see any defaulters of loan. The forum slowly took up educational role through experiential sharing sessions, educative trips and by attending educational camps.

It was realised that common man/woman in particular, acts in faith and that is the driving force for him/her. This faith needs to be properly directed by the more learned people.

Characteristics

(i) Affordable and accessible: It is due to fact that families enrolling for health insurance contribute according to capacity but services are provided according to need, *(ii)* Acceptable: The evidence - more than 95 per cent enrol in the village. It speaks of its quality. All indoor hospitalisation from adopted village occur in Kasturba Hospital, Sevagram. They do not go to the flourishing private health sector in Wardha town. *(iii)* Effective: The evidence—no preventable maternal mortality in past 15 years; no death due to non-accessibility of

medical care; no tetanus, polio, whooping cough, measles in last 15 years; measles is the most sensitive indicator of herd immunity achieved; no misutilization of resources. *(iv)* Accountable: The social finance has generated right to demand, which keeps the service providers of their toes, *(v)* Holistic: It is not an experiment planned from ivory towers with a tubular vision. The experiment has evolved with the involvement and feedback from the people and has transcended holistically to the priority needs of the people, *(vi)* Credible: It is something that cannot be quantified but has to be felt. It can be witnessed in - late night village meetings where discussions turn in to educative sessions; self-help groups not only as a transparent financing body but transforming into a educative forum and empowering women; vastraswavalamban (khadi for own use) and sustainable agricultural practices as a step towards freedom from exploitative market. Self-reliance in priority needs is a key to empowerment *(vii)* Trustworthy: The gains of this experiment have been the relationship of a friend/partner, the free lines of communication with the beneficiary—and the conversion to a big family. There is implicit trust involved and this enables the poor to share their pathos. They come to health care professional with the belief that they would do their best and leave the rest to destiny. A relationship of trust is thus established which brings people together and keeps the scheme going on. *(viii)* Replicability: The credibility of scheme revolves around the will of the hospital management to support. Jajoo was a pivot around which the scheme revolve. In his absence the need based health insurance scheme would continue, though the outreach activities and other dimensions of health would suffer.

The service to the people was main concern. Research was not really a focus because of lack of interested manpower. The focus was instead on operational research and on extending the scheme to community by emphasising other dimensions related to health ethics. Over the years, the scheme has generated a lot of data but this needs to be analysed.

Operational Aspects

The hospital has now become much more accessible to the community and this has helped bring down the incidence of deaths like that due to pneumonia and diarrhoea. Vaccine preventable illnesses (tetanus, polio, whooping cough, measles) have disappeared once herd immunity was established and maintained by cluster approach to immunisation. From the year (1995) government adopted cluster approach to immunisation, vaccination is left to government ANM. The village worker performs a watchdog function to see that all eligible receive it.

The deliveries are free in the hospital for primipara women and for complicated pregnancy. The women can choose to have delivery either in the villages assisted by traditional birth attendant (TEA) or in the hospital. The services now being accessible, women choose to have hospital delivery. ANC (antenatal care) up to seventh month are handled by village health worker. Around the seventh month of pregnancy, women report to Kasturba Hospital for assessment of pelvis, toxaemia and for receiving booster of tetanus toxoid. The area catered by health insurance scheme has not witnessed preventable maternal mortality in the last 15 years and the natal/perinatal mortality has reduced significantly.

The monthly ANC visits in the villages have been given up. ANM visits villages once in three months, checking all records maintained by village workers (ANC registration, vaccination, births, and deaths). With appropriate strategy for vaccination and antenatal care, which utilises village based manpower to the maximum, the need of skilled manpower is reduced to the obligatory minimum. The ANM under the scheme acts at the second tier managing the administrative work of all the villages in addition to supervision of village-based activities in 40 villages. She visits all hospitalized patients, assures expeditious services, entertains their complaints, keeps records and informs tricky problems to the head.

The process of selection of VHW has undergone a sea change. Initially TBA was preferred with a notion that she has natural access to pregnant women and newborns. She belongs to lowest socio-economic class, is needy, hence would be most appropriate choice. The experiences were contrary. She was called only for conducting delivery and taking care of new born for next 10 days since nobody else would do it. She did not and does not enjoy enough credibility in the minds of people. She had to take permission from her husband to accompany a patient in the night to the hospital, if emergency so demands.

The option shifted towards a male member. With the evolving role of VHW, a person with leadership qualities, one who is respected in the community and has aptitude to serve, happened to be the choice. Since the village fund that could be raised from prepayments did not permit lucrative honorarium (it is hardly Rs. 1,000-1,500 per year), only a person from middle class background with aptitude to serve could be selected.

Since the selection was done in consultation with wise and elderly men and women of different caste groups in the village, often in front of the temple, the person acceptable to all had to be one beyond village party-politics.

With SHG movement taking shape, it was easy to locate women with leadership potentiality and serving aptitude. Most of the villages, at present have two village workers, one male and other female, assisting each other for the comprehensive development of village.

As the vision behind the scheme was ever evolving, Ulhas Jajoo, the ANM and village workers all underwent problem based learning. Frequent meetings (often late night) with gram sabha generated directions on which way to go. At no time, need for a formal training was experienced. The team learned by doing and experiential sharing. Everything needed had to be learned by all. The learning transcended beyond scientific to socio-economic-political-spiritual dimensions of life.

According to Ulhas Jajoo, the propagated glorified role of VHW as a liberator in late 1980s and early 1990s had to settle down to ground realities. For peripheral health workers to perform successfully, an effective back-up referral system needed to be in place. The credibility, ultimately in the community is for curative care and not preventive care. The experience in Sevagram has shown that the acceptability of VHW depends greatly on how much support the medical team can extend as a link between the community and health delivery system (PRIA study 1986).

Community involvement is a glibly used slogan. It has different shades—*(i)* community complacence where community is a passive receiver; *(ii)* community cooperation—where manpower support is offered by community; *(iii)* community partnership—demands material support from the community in addition. In all these, there is a 'big brother' that dictates and *(iv)* community participation is a politicised concept. The decision-making lies with the people. There is a common feeling and hence spontaneity in action.

Health being a service sector, professional relationship runs on vertical lines. The health insurance scheme has 'horizontalised' this relationship to the extent possible. It exemplifies health for the people. Sevagram could achieve community partnership while evolving models like 'one house one latrine scheme', milk cooperatives and lift irrigation cooperatives. The scheme did succeed in unifying village community through income generation programmes. But money brought with it liquor, gambling, party politics, police and judicial courts. The fact brought home the painful realisation that pooling people together for material gain is not development.

Villages around Sevagram have witnessed community participation emerging during farmer's movements. It breathed its last because it aimed only for material gain.

The scheme experienced the right kind of community parti-pation emerging with vastraswavalamban yojana, sustainable gricultural practices and SHG movement of women in particular is an empowering experience, evidenced by the anti-liquor lovement that is taking roots in village around Sevagram. The light kind of community participation emerges when spiritual visdom leads and lights.

Experiential Wisdom of the Last 20 Years

For pro-people (poor) health services, self reliance is a myth. The jowar scheme could raise around 10 per cent of what is spent, by social finance. The private insurance which works on the principle of financial risk sharing on no loss basis can never cater to the poor.

It is possible to offer just primary health care to all within presently allotted government resources (250 Rs/per capita year). The maldistribution of centrally pooled resources is what primarily ails our system. The percolation theory—that centrally allotted funds will reach the periphery—fails. If the government decides to hand-over its per capita expenditure on health directly to gram sabha then there can be better control of the health services. Where they control health finances, they can negotiate services from the providers; it gives them a better pedestal. The community can then buy the services from the public or the voluntary sector which is arguably pro-people. Empowerment of people without ownership of resources is not possible. The bottleneck of Sevagram experiment was the fact that people did not own resources and were on receiving end and hence the programme remained vertical and complete participation was not possible.

It requires a radical political will to truly decentralise up to panchayat raj system and distributing resources to it on per capita basis. The structural adjustments of this kind can see the replication of Sevagram experiment. Short of these structural adjustments, wherever 90 per cent of the finances can be granted to the voluntary sector (as is the case of Kasturba Health Society), mechanisms and Organizational part of the scheme would be replicable.

We live in a society where "all men are equal, but some are more equal than others"! It is not an egalitarian society, social relationships are exploitative.

Mere availability of public facility does not make it accessible to 'have-nots': In a democratic society, 'more equal' (haves) have to be restrained, for public benefits to percolate down. It calls for appropriate structural adjustments. The Sevagram village health insurance scheme idolises health care for the people.

The health insurance scheme is unique reaches out to the unorganized sector, poorest of poor—It is the lone health care experiment, which considers village as a social unit and adopts villages. Thereby it attempts to empower the gram sabha in panchayat raj system. It raises social finance and evolves a relationship with the people by talking 'with them' and not talking 'at them'. The vision behind this experiment comes from our role model—Vinoba Bhave who dreamed of an ideal society—a society based on principles of freedom and fraternity, i.e., gram swarajya.

The ethos of the whole process of the scheme's evolution is to develop a democratic society, especially revolving round the village as a unit of society. The concept of village republic (gram swarajya) as envisaged by Gandhi-Vinoba-Jaiprakash Narayan, is the ultimate vision of the scheme. The power lies with the gram sabha which consists of one adult male and female member of each family in the village. It is the highest decision-making body. The decisions are needed to be taken by near consensus. The leaders are selected and not elected. It is in sharp contrast to the panchayati raj system which has in place narrowly elected (51 per cent against 49 per cent) group of representatives. The representative democratic structure is not pro-people in true sense and here it has been replaced by participatory democratic structure of gram sabha.

The concept is detailed under the Gramadan Act of the Indian Constitution that was engineered by Vinoba. Under this act, at least 75 per cent of the population of the village should transfer the title of their land to gram sabha, then only such a village be called as gramadan village. The villagers enjoy the right to plough, cultivate and consume the produce (crop) from the land. However, the land cannot be sold to anybody outside the village. They decide their own land records. Under this act, ownership is collective, but the individuals continue to enjoy consumption right over fruits of their labour for generations to come. Thus it promotes a society which survives on, 'bread labour' and does not permit 'intellectual labour' to exploit. The ideal society would be one that would revolve around concept of 'bread labour'. In such society there would not be much difference between the members and interdependence will be obligatory. The decision-making then would be a collective exercise which would decrease the possibility of unfair or wrong decisions.

Empowering the gram sabha is the key to gram swarajya. Empowerment occurs when resources are owned and freedom of decision-making rests with gram sabha, when decision-making is obligatorily by consensus or overwhelming majority, no wrong decisions can occur.

How should health system be in the context of gram swarajya? It has to be health by the people, for the people and of the people. Since the resources must be owned by gram sabha, the Sevagram experiment proposes distribution of centrally-pooled resources by the state and central governments to be distributed back to village on per capita basis. Also the freedom of which services to buy—should also rest with gram sabha so that 'just' decisions can evolve. Short of these structural adjustments (which requires strong political will), Kasturba Hospital, Sevagram holds the government grants in trust and distributes public money appropriately by raising a model of health for the people.

Jowar health insurance scheme at Sevagram is an attempt to identify revered individuals (sajjan shakti), to empower by bringing them together, inculcate a culture of decision-making by consensus and initiate acts of common faith.

Looking back at the experiment that this scheme has been, a model indeed has been developed, which is ideal and is replicable in an ideal kind of society envisaged. The lamp needs to keep burning until the fire catches on. This is a 'micro' experiment for a 'macro' ideal. The need is to act locally, while thinking globally.

ACCORD Community Health Insurance Increasing Access to Hospital Care

In India, while 5 per cent of GDP is spent on health, the government contributes only 0.9 per cent towards it or less than Rs 100 per capita per year. Internationally, this is one of the lowest health expenditures by any government. More than 80 per cent of most government budgets are earmarked for salaries. This means that there are very little funds for drugs, programmes and other activities. And finally there is an inequitable allocation of health resources, about 30 per cent of the government health budget is used by the richest quintile while the poorest quintile gets only 10 per cent [Peters et al 2002]. These under-funded government health services thus provides poor quality of care. Common complaints include poor utilization of the primary health care facilities, overcrowding at the secondary and tertiary health care facilities, lack of adequate manpower, drugs and equipment [Gupte 1993]. This causes most patients to shift over to the private sector for health care. About 85 per cent of patients use the private sector for ambulatory care, while 40-60 per cent use the private sector for inpatient care [Peters et al 2002].

Using the private sector in India implies out-of-pocket expenditure at the time of illness. This may have two outcomes—either the patient does not access care or the patient accesses care but is impoverished in the process [Kawabata et al 2002]. Utilization studies in India have reported hospitalisation rates in the range of 15 to 20 hospitalisations per 1,000 population [Sundar and Sharma 2002, Ranson 2002, Raman 1996], However, this is considerably lower than African and Asian figures [Criel et al 1998]. Those who do access care are pushed below the poverty line. Studies have shown that more than 40 per cent of hospitalisation patients borrow money or sell assets to meet medical costs. In the process, an average of 24 per cent of hospitalized patients become impoverished [Peters et al 2002]. Thus it appears that India's poor have problems with accessing hospital care. And those who do access health care have the risk of falling into iatrogenic poverty poverty [Meessen et al 2003]. One possible solution to this problem is to reduce the financial barrier through health insurance. Unfortunately, currently only about 10 per cent of the population is protected under any health insurance coverage. Of this, most are for employees in the formal sector [Ellis et al 2000]. The informal sector is totally unprotected and has to depend on the aforementioned poorly financed public sector or the expensive private sector to take care of its needs. The government is keen to increase the insurance coverage and has even introduced special health insurance packages for the poor ('Pay-off Time for NDA on Penson, Health Schemes', *The Times of India,* July 14, 2003). However, these initiatives have not been acceptable to the citizens of this country ('Concern over Low overall Health Insurance Focus', *The Economic Times,* December 9, 2003).

In this context, a few voluntary Organizations have developed community health insurance (CHI) schemes to meet the health financing needs of the poor [Ranson 2003]. Through a prepayment and risk pooling mechanism, the poor are able to meet their health needs with minimum burden at the time of use. However, while currently there are more than 20 such schemes in our country [Ranson et al 2003], there is very little empirical evidence about their performance. We describe here one such scheme managed by Action for Community Organization, Rehabilitation and Development (ACCORD), the Adivasi Munnetra Sangam (AMS) and the Association for Health Welfare in the Nilgiris (ASHWINI). We first describe the ACCORD-AMS-ASHWINI'(AAA) CHI scheme in detail and look at its performance vis-a-vis access to hospitalisation. We finally look at some of the determinants of this performance and come up with recommendations for improved performance of CHI schemes.

We studied the AAA CHI programme and reviewed its performance over the past 11 years. Interviews with key informants provided the qualitative information; while secondary data from records, registers and reports provided the quantitative data:

Principal Findings ACCORD-AMS-ASHWINI (AAA)

ACCORD is a local non-governmental Organization (NGO) staffed by a group of professionals and adivasi youth. Established in 1986, it works exclusively for indigenous groups, or 'the adivasis', of Gudalur taluk, Nilgiris district, Tamil Nadu. ACCORD's main objective is to empower the 15,000 plus adivasis of Gudalur to protect their rights. This ranges from land to forest rights. ACCORD also provides services like health, education, agricultural support and housing. The AMS is a federation of village level unions ('sanghas').'The main objective of the village sangham and the AMS is to defend the rights of adivasis. The AMS also takes responsibility for the development of all the adivasis in Gudalur. ASHWINI manages the health programme today. The health programme consists of a two-tier structure—a network of seven health centres, manned by medical assistants and a 20-bed hospital with all basic facilities, including obstetrics and surgery. The health centres provide a mixture of curative and preventive care. Most of the villages also have trained village health workers who provide basic health care to their community. ACCORD initiated and developed the health programme and' handed it over to a sister NGO—ASHWINI in 1998. ASHWINI is staffed and managed by adivasi youth. AAA CHI—History and Design: During the period 1987-1990, because of community health work, the demand for health care grew among the adivasis. While initially ACCORD tried to use the existing government and private health care facilities, they were found to be wanting in many aspects. A hospital for the adivasis became an increasing demand of the adivasi community. Prolonged discussions with the community always ended with the question:—"How will this-venture be funded?" The people agreed to contribute a certain amount towards the cost of running the hospital.

Keeping this promise in mind, the Adivasi Hospital was inaugurated in December 1990. ACCORD realised that user fees were inequitable and explored the possibility of insuring the adivasis. Many General Insurance Companies (GIC) companies were contacted, but only New India Assurance Corporation (NIAC) evinced some interest. Negotiations with them over a period of a year resulted in the development of a new package—the 'Composite Tribal Health Insurance Package', which was launched in March 1992. Its main objectives are given in Box. This programme (called AAA CHI here) has been operational for the past 12 years, the initial 10 years with NIAC and the last year with the Royal Sundaram Alliance Private Limited (RSA). The three main stakeholders—ACCORD, AMS and ASHWINI, manage the AAA CHI programme.

As the NIAC package did not meet all the needs of the adivasi community, AAA introduced some changes to make it more acceptable to the community. Thus the AAA CHI should be seen at two levels—one provided by the NIAC to AAA and the other by AAA to the adivasi community. The AAA CHI is depicted in Figure 1. The basic elements are as follows: The community: Only adivasis-residing in Gudalur taluk who are AMS members are eligible for the scheme. There are about 12,000 plus AMS members, of which only those between six months to sixty years are eligible to enrol as per the NIAC guidelines. These adivasis are traditionally hunter-gatherers and have been classified by the Government of India as 'primitive tribal groups' because of their pre-agricultural economy, low literacy rates and dwindling population. Today most of them are engaged as casual labourers in the tea estates and earn an average of about Rs 1000 (US$22) per family per month. This income has been threatened in the past three to four years, due to the fall in tea leaf prices.

The premium: The premium has to be seen at two distinct levels. In 1992, ACCORD negotiated with NIAC to insure all the AMS members for a period of five years. This enabled AAA to avail of the long-term discount as well as group discount. Additionally, the AAA limited the benefit package to a maximum of Rs 1,500 per person per year. All this reduced the annual premium from Rs 48 to Rs 13 per person per year. As the adivasis were not able to pay the lump sum of Rs 260 per household (equivalent to a quarter of their monthly income), AAA negotiated the following package with them. ACCORD agreed to pay the entire amount upfront to NIAC. The adivasi community agreed to repay this amount as annual instalments to ACCORD. The AMS took the responsibility of collecting the premium.

ACCORD thus paid the premium of Rs 65 per adivasi and covered 5,995 adivasis in the first round. The lump sum amount of Rs 3,86,318 was provided by CEBEMO, a Dutch funding agency. New members who joined subsequently were enrolled on a pro-rata basis. The scheme was renewed in 1997 for another five-year period; once again CEBEMO/BILANCE helped meet the lump sum payment of Rs 523,110 to insure 9786 tribals for five years. In 2002, NIAC hiked the premium by a substantial amount, so AAA approached Royal Sundaram Alliance Private Limited. They agreed to provide hospitalisation coverage upto a limit of Rs 1000 for a premium of Rs 20 per person per year. The AMS members have been insured for a year from 2003-2004.

In the initial years, as insurance was a new concept, the premium was heavily subsidised. In 1992, no premium was collected from the community. In 1993, AMS members were asked to repay at Rs. 4 per person. In the next year, this was raised to Rs. 6 per person, and in 1995 Rs. 8 was collected. Thus by the year 1997, the entire annual premium amount was being paid by the adivasis. In the subsequent years, the premium amount was raised and in 2002 they paid Rs. 22 per person. Thus while AAA insured the tribals en masse with a formal insurance company and paid their premiums for five years, the tribals repaid this premium on an annual basis.

The premium is a community rated one and the unit of enrolment is the individual. It is usually collected once a year between December 5th (Adivasi day) and April 15th (Vishu). These dates are important on the tribal calendar and coincide with the coffee plucking season, when the demand for labour is high. While initially the AMS leaders and the ACCORD staff went from house to house to collect the premium, today a considerable part of it is collected at central collection points. An insurance card, with details of name, age, gender, village name and the unique AMS membership number, is given annually to those who repay. This card is valid for one year from April 15th to April 14th of the next year.

The money gathered at the collection centres as well as details of those insured is handed over to the hospital accountant once a month. At the end of the collection period, AAA shares the information about premium collection with the adivasi community, including villagewise details about numbers insured and the amount collected. The details of AMS members enrolled by AAA and those who have repaid annually are shown in Figure 2. The insurers: AAA reinsures the tribals with a formal insurance company, who is the prime insurer of this scheme. From 1992 to 2002. It was the New India Assurance Company (MAC) and in 2003. It was the Royal Sundaram Alliance Private Limited. This reinsurance mechanism increases the risk pool for the community. The providers: ASHWINI is the main provider of health care. As stated earlier, it has a network of health centres and a hospital. It refers patients to tertiary centres at Kozhikode or Coimbatore when necessary. ASHWINI's staff are predominantly adivasis themselves. It uses strategies like paying fixed salaries, and using essential drugs and standard treatment guidelines to keep the costs low. The average hospital bill is about Rs 750 per patient per episode of illness (2001). Less than 10 per cent of claims cross the Rs 1,500 limit. Also the adivasi management committee ensures that the care provided is acceptable to the community. While the health centres are open only for adivasi patients, the hospital admits non-tribals also. The non-tribals pay a fee for service, which is higher than the actual costs and helps cross-subsidise some of the services for the adivasis. The benefit package: The benefit package has to be viewed at two levels. A package provided by the insurance company to AAA and another (more comprehensive) provided by AAA to the adivasis. NIAC assured only hospital care with an upper limit of Rs 1,500 per patient per year. This included most common ailments but excluded pre-existing and self-inflicted illnesses as well as diseases due to substance abuse. Deliveries and family planning operations were initially excluded. However, while renewing the policy in 1997, AAA managed to include the first two deliveries and family, planning operations into the benefit package. All admissions were to be for more than 24 hours and in the ASHWINI hospital. In 2003, RSA maintained the same benefit package, but the maximum limit was reduced to Rs 1,000 per patient per year. Only psychiatric illnesses were excluded and reimbursement is through an indemnity mechanism.

In 1992, there was additional coverage for damage to hut and personal accident coverage for the head of the household. However, this was removed in 1997 as AMS felt it was not very beneficial. This further reduced the premium.

While this was the benefit package provided by the insurance companies, AAA offered a more comprehensive package to the adivasi community. For those who repaid the premium, outpatient (OP) services (including medicines and diagnostics) at the Adivasi Hospital were provided for a small co-payment of Rs lO per visit.

There were no exclusions for hospitalisation. And there were no upper limits. Also the insured patient did not have to pay anything at the time of discharge. The non-insured patient had to meet the cost of OP medicines and pay Rs 100 for every hospitalisation. ASHWINI also provides promotive, preventive and basic curative care through its network of voluntary health workers (VHWs) and health centres. This benefit is provided to all AMS members, irrespective of their insurance status. As AAA provides comprehensive care it encourages people to live a healthy life and to seek care at the earliest when ill so that problems are addressed close to home, at the area centre or at the hospital. This cuts down morbidity and expenses. While theoretically the patient has to be referred by the health centre for admission, in reality this is not adhered to very strictly. Thus while the formal insurance company provides a hospitalisation package, AAA uses its resources to provide a more holistic cover. External resources, as well as the profits generated from non-tribal patients meet the difference in the benefit package.

Claims and reimbursements: Claims and reimbursements are simplified considerably. At the end of hospitalisation, three copies of the hospital bill are made. One copy is handed over to the patient (but the patient does not pay any amount). The second copy is kept for records and the third is forwarded by ASHWINI to the insurance company (on a monthly basis). Any hospitalisation for an excluded illness is not claimed by ASHWINI. Similarly claims are made only to a maximum of Rs 1,500. The insurance company in turn reimburses ASHWINI on a regular basis, usually after a lag time of three to six months. The reimbursement rates have been in the range of 95-100 per cent. The administration: ACCORD, AMS and ASHWINI mainly administer the AAA CHI. ASHWINI and ACCORD field staff as well as the AMS leaders collect the premium. The field staff has other work and collecting premium is an additional responsibility that they have undertaken. The AMS leaders do the same on a voluntary basis. A system of receipts and strict accounting, measures prevents fraud. The ASHWINI accountant processes the claims and submits it to the NIAC/RSA. The patient does not have to provide any documentation, except to bring along the insurance card at the time of admission. Feedback to the community is provided by ACCORD/ASHWINI every year. Risk management: Adverse selection is kept to a minimum by encouraging the family to enrol as a unit and by having a definite collection period. Moral hazard is also minimised by a system of co-payments. Also the indirect costs of transport, food and loss of wages are a significant barrier to unnecessary hospitalisations.

Paying the provider a fixed salary rather than a fee for service helps contain provider induced moral hazard. Figure 3 shows how the average cost per patient has remained steady over the years. Cost recovery: This health insurance programme has been functioning over the past 12 years. It has mobilised revenue from both the community and donors. Table 1 shows the sources of income and expenditure in the year 1999-2000. Sixty per cent of hospitalisation costs are recovered through the insurance programme. However, this is a slight overestimate, as one also needs to factor in the outpatient and administration costs and unfortunately these figures were not available. The difference in the claims and reimbursements are mainly due to exclusions and also because 58 of the claims exceeded the Rs 1,500 limit. Donors and cross subsidy from non-tribal patients meet the deficit of Rs 2.36 lakhs.

Performance vis-a-vis Utilization of Hospital Services

Hospitalisation was assessed from hospital records. The hospitalisation rate among those who have repaid the premium and those who have not paid the premium is shown in Figure 4. As can be seen, the insured use the hospital four times more than the non-insured. This was higher in the initial years, but has stabilised over the past years. Admission rates by distance show a gentle curve (Figure 5). There appears to be an increased utilization of hospital services by .those living in the middle distance. Table 2 shows the top five reasons for admission in both the insured and non-insured populations. The main reasons for admission in both groups are communicable diseases -respiratory and gastrointestinal infections. Deliveries and associated illnesses are another major reason for admission. And finally the admission rates by income quartiles are given in Table 3. From this table it appears that the utilization is uniform in the three lower quartiles.

Discussion

Very few Indians are protected by any form of social security, especially health insurance, and most patients are forced to pay from their pocket to access quality care. This financial barrier lowers access to health care. Health insurance, by its pre-payment and risk pooling mechanisms-, theoretically reduces the financial barriers, thereby improving access. One of the main functions of health insurance is to increase access to health care [Kutzin 1998].

Unfortunately in India, only about 10 percent of the population (and that too, employees of the formal sector) are covered under any form of health insurance. However, voluntary Organizations have been developing mechanisms to insure the poor in the informal sector against high cost health events. Currently there are more than 20 such schemes. These 'community health insurance schemes' are small ventures organized by voluntary Organizations and encourage people to pre-pay for future health events. This results in risk pooling

—between the healthy and the sick. While there have been various descriptive narrations about these CHIs [Ranson 2003], their performance has rarely been assessed. SEWA (in Ahmedabad) is one exception, where the effect of insurance on utilization of health services [Ranson 2001], catastrophic health expenditure [Ranson 2002] and quality of care [Ranson et al 2003] have been studied. In these studies, the author concludes that there is not much increase in utilization of health service due to insurance, that insurance has a protective effect against catastrophic health expenditure and that insurance does not ensure better quality of care.

In this article, we look at just one aspect of performance-utilization of health services. There appears to be a higher utilization of health care by those insured in the AAA CHI programme. From the data, it is clear that those who have subscribed to the insurance programme have used the hospital services much more than the non-insured. Considering the poverty of this population and the relatively high cost of hospital services, this AAA CHI seems to have overcome the financial barrierto accessing hospital care. It's effect is even seen over geographical distances. The data on admissions by distance shows that the gradient is relatively gentle, indicating that health insurance was able to overcome some of the normal effects of distance on utilization. What is surprising is that those who access health care the most, appear to be those residing in the middle distance—within 5-35 kms. This is surprising but may be explained by the fact that people who live nearby access the services early enough and so do not need hospitalisation.

Table 1: Cost Recovery of Community Health Insurance Programme, 1999-2000

Income	*Rs*	*Expenditure*	*Rs*
Premium collected from 4649tribals @ Rs15per person per year.	69.735	Premium paid to the NIAC for 11585 tribals @ Rs 13 per tribal per year	150605
Reimbursement from the NIAC for 586 patients	276467	Cost of treating 657patients @ Rs 658 per patient	432306
Total	346202	Total	582911

Table 2: Admission Patterns Among the Insured and Non-Insured, 1999

Diagnosis	*No. of Insured Admitted (%age of all Insured Admissions)*	*No. of Non-Insured Admitted (%age of all Non-Insured Admissions)*
Acute lower respiratory infections	93(14.6)	49(22.9)
Deliveries	74(11.6)	29(13.5)
Diarrhoea + Dysentery	55 (8.6)	23(10.8)
Injuries	37 (5.8)	4(6.5)
Typhoid fever	33 (5.2)	3(1.4)
TB	27 (4.3)	13(6.5)

Table 3: Hospitalisation Rates Per 1000 Adivasis by Economic Status

Economic status	*Total Population*	*Insured*	*Non-Insured*
Q1	410	68.3	34.1
Q2	7460	51.3	19.6
Q3	3180	69.2	12.6
Q4	644	12.4	15.5

Source : Census of India 1991.

The utilization rates of health services are much higher, than those documented in India [NSSO 1998]. One explanation for this here could be adverse selection or patient induced moral hazard. Adverse selection would imply that people who have a higher probability of illness (e.g., those suffering from chronic illness) insure at a higher rate as compared to others. A proxy indicator for this would be the average length of stay - which would be higher among patients with chronic illnesses than with others. However, Figure 6 clearly shows that this is not so. The insured have a lower length of stay (mean = 3.92 days) as compared to the non-insured (mean = 4.50 days). This is further reinforced by the top five reasons for admission, which indicate that both the insured and the non-insured appear to have similar illnesses. Thus adverse selection may be ruled out to a certain extent. This is understandable considering that steps have been introduced in the design to prevent adverse selection. Moral hazard by the patient may be a possibility, though the indirect costs (transport and food) are so high, that it should effectively pre-empt patients from unnecessarily seeking health care. The lower length of stay among the insured also indicates that they may be seeking health care earlier and so getting cured earlier. This would be one more argument to indicate that health insurance does improve access to health care.

While African studies have shown that CHIs have increased access to health care [Criel et al 1999, Baeza et al 2002, Atim 1998], a study from India showed that there was no such effect [Cumber and Kulkarni 2000]. This current study thus is the first to show a positive impact of CHI on utilization of services in India. This is all the more important if one keeps in mind that the community is one of the poorest—adivasis in a remote corner of the country.

One of the other achievements of the AAA CHI has been the ability to mobilise community resources. The AAA has been able to tap into the enormous social capital that is available in the community. Volunteers have helped with time and staff have contributed by taking on extra responsibility. Sixty per cent of the hospitalisation costs of insured patients have been recovered through the insurance programme. This is a significant amount. Unfortunately, accurate figures on the outpatient and the preventive care programme were not available. This would have given a more precise idea about the exact cost and the subsidy required. This has policy implications as it can spell out the per capita subsidy required to make a CHI financially sustainable.

Health insurance is considered to be an equitable form of health financing. While private health insurance has the potential to increase inequities [Mahal 2002], CHI by its limited risk pooling does not enhance equity either. While there is risk pooling between the healthy and the sick, there is practically none between the rich and the poor. This is because the target population are the poor only. This can be rectified if other sections of society are enrolled into the CHI. This would of course mean catering to the needs of a more varied section of society, which has it's inherent problems. Another way to enhance equity is through reinsurance, wherein a formal insurance company amalgamates smaller and dedicated risk pools. This is what was done in the AAA CHI. The adivasi risk pool was enlarged by linking it with the NIAC's pool.

While the AAA CHI seems to have increased access to care, we describe here some of the determinants for this performance. One major determinant is that the CHI was introduced within the context of an overall development intervention. ACCORD was engaged in various development initiatives and the CHI was part of this. It was also built on the existing foundation of solidarity; the AMS had initiated a movement in which adivasis supported each other in times of need. The CHI was thus seen as an intervention where the healthy assisted the sick. And finally, the AMS was involved from the beginning in the design and implementation of the AAA CHI. So there was a sense of ownership, which helped sustain the programme over the years. In fact the CHI grew out of a felt need of the adivasi community to contribute towards hospital expenses. While other voluntary agencies or hospitals may not have this luxury, they could piggyback health insurance activities on existing group activities, e.g., micro credit or the cooperatives.

The second issue was one of affordability. While the initial package was beyond the reach of this poor community, negotiations helped in making it more affordable and allowed the community to contribute regularly. This was further assisted by the initial subsidy until the community became aware of health insurance and its benefits. One worrying aspect about the adivasi subscription is that only about 40-50 per cent of the AMS members have enrolled at any point in time. And over the years, this has been reducing. Discussions with the staff and community reveal various reasons. One of the reasons stated is the steadily worsening local economy: it has resulted in a diminished cash flow. The other reason is the issue of distance. Those who reside further away from the hospital find that the indirect costs of transporting a patient to the ASHWINI hospital offsets any benefit obtained from insurance.

Yet another reason for the programme to 'succeed' was the creation of a benefit package that suited the needs of the people. While the NIAC benefit package was a typical "Mediclaim" package, AAA added further elements to it to make it more comprehensive: free outpatient care at the hospital, removal of exclusions, cashless hospitalisation and no upper limit. All of these helped make health insurance more acceptable. While premium with a large benefit package, one needs to see health insurance not just from an economic point of view. Health insurance plays important health system functions also: increased access to health care and the protection of households from impoverishment at the time of illness [Kutzin 1998]. Thus for a CHI to be effective, it is imperative that the benefit package is tailored to meet the needs of the community. And ideally the providers should be acceptable to the community, in the case of the AAA CHI, the AMS managed the health programme. This plus the high quality of care provided by the programme made it very acceptable to the adivasi community.

One of the pillars of any CHI is the administration. Village volunteers, using existing community platforms, create awareness about insurance and collect the premium. The claims and reimbursements are managed with minimum documentation. However, this does not mean that the administration is lax—strict accounting and review processes ensure that fraud is practically absent. Regular feedback and transparency ensures that the individual is aware of the purpose that his/her contribution was used for.

One of the major limitations of this study is that we relied only on secondary data from the Gudalur Adivasi Hospital. This meant that we missed out on patients (especially non-insured) who sought care in other health institutions. Thus the gap in utilization, between the insured and the non-insured, is actually smaller than, portrayed here.

Conclusions

The poor in India need to be protected from high out-of-pocket expenditures on health. A well-managed pre-payment system with risk pooling is effective in removing financial barriers at the time of illness. This can increase access to care, an important step towards improving the health status of households. Community health insurance is an innovative method to extend social protection to excluded groups. However for this to happen, community health insurance needs to start on the foundation of solidarity, to have an affordable premium, an appropriate benefit package and a minimal administrative burden. Provision of health care is a major issue, and the agency needs to negotiate with the providers for measures to contain cost and maintain quality.

Bibliography

Akerlof, G. (1970): 'The Market for 'Lemons': Qualitative Uncertainty and the Market Mechanism', *Quarterly Journal of Economics,* 84, pp. 488-500.

Arrow, K. (1963): 'Uncertainty and the Welfare Economcis of Medical care', *American Economic Review,* 53 (5), pp. 941-73.

Bhat, R. (1996): 'Regulation of the Private Health Sector in India', *International Journal of Health planning and Management,* 11, pp. 253-74.

Burges, R.N. Stern (1991): 'Social Security in Developing Countries: What, Why, Who, and How? In Dreze Ahmed, Sen Hills (eds.), *Social Security in Developing Countries, Wider Studies in Development Economics,* Clarendon Press, Oxford, pp. 41-80.

Ellis, Randall, Moneer Alam and Indrani Gupta (2000): 'Health Insurance in India : Prognosia and prospectus'. *Economics and Political weekly,* vol. XXXV. No. 4. January 22-28.

Mahal, Ajay (2000): Who benefit from public sector health spending in India? Results of benefit incidence analysis, National Council of Applied Economic Research.

Nandraj, Sunil and Anagha Khot (2003): Accreditation system for health facilities: Challenges and opportunities, *Economics and Political Weekly,* vol. xxxviii, No. 50. December 13-19.

Peters, D.H. (2000) : Introduction conclusions in peters D.H (ed), private health insurance and public health goals in India, report on a national seminar, World Bank, May, New Delhi.

Peters, D.H. Yazbeck A.S., Sharma R., Ramana, G.N.V., Pritchett, Wagslaff A (2002): Better Health Systems for India's Poor: Findings, Analysis, and Options, World Bank, Washington DC.

Ranson, K. and M. Jowett (2003): Developing Health indusrance in India, Background paper to the Government of India Workshop on Health Insurance, January 3-4, New Delhi.

Simonm, Nayan (2000): 'Role of TPAs in Health Insurance', presentation at two-day conference on Health Insurance in India', Indian Institute of Management, March 18-19.

Simon, S.R. (2001): 'Views of Managed Care—A Study of Students, Residents, Faculty, and Deans at Medical Schools in the United States. *The New England Journal of Medicine,* 340, pp. 928-36.

Sonderstrom, L. (1997): 'The Idea of social protection', in *Sustaining Social Security,* United Nations, New York, pp. 43-73.

Spence, M. (1973) : 'Job Marketing signalling', *Quarterly Journal of Economics*, 87, pp. 355-74.

Tulasidhar, V.B. (1996) : Public financing for health in India : Recent trends, International Health Policy Programme, Washington.

Visaria, P. and A. Gumber (1994): Utilization of and expenditure on health care in India, 1986-87, Gujarat Institute of Development Research, Ahmedabad,

World Health Organization (2000): The World Health Report 2000: Health Systems: Improving Performance, WHO, Geneva.

Yip, W. and P. Berman (2001): Targeted Health Insurance in a Low income country and its impact on Access and Equity in Access, Egypt's Social Health Insurance, *Health Economics*, 10: 207-20.